Glenn (
930 Fair
Ojai, California 93023

THE BOOK OF MOSES
and the
JOSEPH SMITH TRANSLATION MANUSCRIPTS

THE BOOK OF MOSES
and the
JOSEPH SMITH TRANSLATION MANUSCRIPTS

Kent P. Jackson

RELIGIOUS STUDIES CENTER
BRIGHAM YOUNG UNIVERSITY

Published by the Religious Studies Center, Brigham Young University,
Provo, Utah

ISBN 0-8425-2589-0

CONTENTS

Old Testament Manuscript 1, page 1, the first page of the Joseph Smith Translation of the Bible, June 1830; handwriting of Oliver Cowdery; Moses 1:1–19

PREFACE

This book is a study of the text of Selections from the Book of Moses, an excerpt of Genesis from the Joseph Smith Translation of the Bible. Commonly called the Book of Moses, it is the first section in the Pearl of Great Price, one of the standard works of scripture of the Church of Jesus Christ of Latter-day Saints.

In June 1830, just two months after the Church was organized, the Prophet Joseph Smith was instructed by the Lord to begin a careful reading of the Bible to revise and make corrections to it as prompted by revelation. His work on the Bible, begun that month at the beginning of Genesis, extended through July 1833. Over the course of three years, the Prophet dictated 446 large manuscript pages to his scribes and made changes in about 3,400 verses of the Bible.[1] Some of the changes consist only of minor editing to the words of the existing King James translation, but other changes are additions of much new material. Today the resulting work is commonly called the Joseph Smith Translation (JST). The title *Inspired Version* refers to the edited, printed edition, published by the Community of Christ (historically, the Reorganized Church of Jesus Christ of Latter Day Saints [RLDS]).[2]

---

1. See Robert J. Matthews, *"A Plainer Translation": Joseph Smith's Translation of the Bible—A History and Commentary* (Provo, UT: Brigham Young University Press, 1975), 424–25.

2. First published in 1867 as *The Holy Scriptures, Translated and Corrected by the Spirit of Revelation. By Joseph Smith, Jr., the Seer.* (Plano, IL: The [Reorganized] Church of Jesus Christ of Latter-Day Saints, 1867). The most recent edition was published in Independence, Missouri, in 1991. In 2001 the RLDS Church changed its name to the Community of Christ.

The Prophet and his contemporaries referred to his Bible revision as the New Translation.[3] The Book of Moses is an excerpt from this work, the New Translation of Genesis 1:1–6:13.

The present study of the Book of Moses consists of three main parts. In "History of the Book of Moses," I summarize briefly the story of the text from its origin in the Joseph Smith Translation through the various manuscripts and printings that constitute its rich and interesting history. In the "Historical Text," I present the text of the Book of Moses as it is recorded on Joseph Smith's final manuscript of this section of the New Translation, what is called Old Testament Manuscript 2. The transcription includes the strikeouts and insertions that document the work of the Prophet and his scribes. Extensive footnotes that identify the scribes and show the history of the words with the variant readings that are found in original manuscripts and later printings accompany the text. Finally, I present the "Manuscript Text" of the Book of Moses, the text as the Prophet Joseph Smith prepared it and left it to the Church. I have added modern spelling, capitalization, and punctuation to the "Manuscript Text." A brief conclusion follows.

When Joseph Smith died in 1844, his widow, Emma Hale Smith, possessed the manuscripts of the New Translation. When the Church moved west with Brigham Young and the Twelve, she retained the manuscripts with her in Illinois, where she preserved them carefully for the next two decades. In the 1860s, the Reorganized Church of Jesus Christ of Latter Day Saints was established. Emma Smith Bidamon put the manuscripts into the care of her son Joseph Smith III, president of the newly established church, and since then they have been protected in RLDS archival facilities. Today they are housed in the Library-Archives of the Community of Christ in Independence, Missouri.

The manuscripts of the Joseph Smith Translation are among the foundational documents of the Restoration. Two excerpts, the Book of Moses and Joseph Smith—Matthew, are parts of our canonized scripture. Unfortunately every Latter-day Saint printing of those texts from the 1851 origi-

---

3. See D&C 124:89; *Times and Seasons* 1, no. 9 (July 1840): 140; Joseph Smith, *History of the Church of Jesus Christ of Latter-day Saints*, ed. B. H. Roberts, 2nd ed. rev. (Salt Lake City: Deseret Book, 1957), 1:341, 365; 4:164.

nal edition of the Pearl of Great Price to the present was accomplished without access to the original manuscripts. Those who worked on the editions could rely at best only on imperfect handwritten or printed copies, or copies of copies, rather than on the texts that were prepared by the Prophet. As a result, in many places the words today differ from how they were left to the Church by Joseph Smith.

In the year 2004, the Religious Studies Center at Brigham Young University published *Joseph Smith's New Translation of the Bible: Original Manuscripts.*[4] That volume includes carefully prepared transcriptions of all the original manuscript pages of the Joseph Smith Translation. Prior to its publication, leaders and members of the Church of Jesus Christ of Latter-day Saints, with very rare exceptions, did not have access to the original documents. Because of the gracious cooperation that Latter-day Saint scholars received from the Community of Christ in preparing that publication of the original manuscripts, Latter-day Saints can now study for themselves the texts as they were dictated by the Prophet Joseph Smith and recorded by his scribes. The access that we now have has allowed us to obtain a much better understanding of many questions relative to the New Translation, including how it was accomplished, who the scribes were, when it was done, and how the text was intended to be read and understood.

Most important is the fact that we now have access to the revealed text itself, which we did not have before, and we can examine the words as they were recorded when they first came from the inspired lips of the Prophet. We are in a new day, a day of closer access to one of the great fruits of the Restoration—an important branch of Joseph Smith's calling, as he designated his inspired work on the Bible.[5] With our ability now to examine the original documents closely, we can express our thanks to a loving God who has provided that "righteousness and truth" would "sweep the earth" in the

---

4. See Scott H. Faulring, Kent P. Jackson, and Robert J. Matthews, eds., *Joseph Smith's New Translation of the Bible: Original Manuscripts* (Provo, UT: Religious Studies Center, Brigham Young University, 2004). The manuscript material in the present volume is based on the transcriptions in Faulring, Jackson, and Matthews, used here with permission.

5. See Joseph Smith, *History of the Church*, 1:238.

last days (Moses 7:62), a loving God who said concerning the Joseph Smith Translation, "The scriptures shall be given, even as they are in mine own bosom, to the salvation of mine own elect" (D&C 35:20).

The images on pages vi, 4, 5, 8, 26, 58, 104, 112, 122, 125, 132, and 141 are courtesy of the Library-Archives, Community of Christ, Independence, Missouri. Images on pages 13, 15, 16, 19, 40, 42, and 44 are courtesy of the L. Tom Perry Special Collections, Harold B. Lee Library, Brigham Young University, Provo, Utah. Images on pages 30, 31, and 32 are courtesy of Dennis A. Wright, Springville, Utah. Images on pages 35, 46, 49, and 51 are courtesy of the author.

This book is not a publication of the Church of Jesus Christ of Latter-day Saints, and the conclusions presented in it are my own. I would like to express my thanks to student assistants who contributed significantly in the preparation of the book and to my wife, Nancy Jackson, without whose efforts it would not have been possible. I express my thanks also to colleagues at Brigham Young University and especially to Robert J. Matthews, for his keen interest in this work and his ongoing counsel and encouragement.

HISTORY OF

THE BOOK OF MOSES

Selections from the Book of Moses in the Pearl of Great Price is the Joseph Smith Translation (JST) of Genesis 1:1–6:13, the beginning pages of the New Translation.[1] The material in it was revealed between June 1830 and February 1831. In some ways, the Book of Moses[2] can be considered the most significant part of the JST, because it has contributed more distinctive Latter-day Saint doctrine than any other part of that work. It has stood since the beginning of the Church of Jesus Christ of Latter-day Saints as one of the doctrinal cornerstones of the Restoration and as an enduring testimony to the divinely inspired work of Joseph Smith.

We are indebted to Elder Franklin D. Richards of the Quorum of the Twelve Apostles for the existence of the Pearl of Great Price and for including the Book of Moses in it. In 1851, while serving as president of the British Mission in Liverpool, England, he prepared a mission pamphlet containing "a choice selection from the revelations, translations, and narrations of Joseph

---

1. Transcriptions of the original manuscript pages, with introductory essays, are presented in Scott H. Faulring, Kent P. Jackson, and Robert J. Matthews, eds., *Joseph Smith's New Translation of the Bible: Original Manuscripts* (Provo, UT: Religious Studies Center, Brigham Young University, 2004). All citations from original manuscripts are from that source.

2. The title "Book of Moses" was first added in 1902. In 1981 the title was made more precise with "Selections from the Book of Moses." For convenience, I will follow the common practice and use "Book of Moses" even in contexts that predate the application of that name in 1902.

Smith."[3] He drew the title, the *Pearl of Great Price*, from the treasured object in Jesus's parable in Matthew 13:45–46. Among other important texts of the Restoration, Elder Richards included excerpts of the first chapters of Genesis from Joseph Smith's Bible translation.[4] Since the 1851 Liverpool publication, other editions of material from the Genesis translation have appeared in print. In 1867 the Reorganized Church of Jesus Christ of Latter Day Saints published what is now commonly called the *Inspired Version*, an edited transcript of the entire JST. That was followed in 1878 by a new edition of the Pearl of Great Price, published by the Church of Jesus Christ of Latter-day Saints in Salt Lake City, Utah. Revised editions of the Pearl of Great Price, each with changes to the text of the Book of Moses, followed in 1902, 1921, and 1981.

Old Testament Manuscript 1

The JST was recorded in ink on the common writing paper of the Prophet's day, "foolscap" paper. The name applies to a size of sheets approximately sixteen by thirteen inches in dimension.[5] They were folded in the middle and stitched at the fold, making writing booklets with pages about eight inches wide and thirteen inches tall. The original dictated text of Joseph Smith's Genesis translation is on a manuscript titled Old Testament

---

3. Franklin D. Richards, *The Pearl of Great Price: Being a Choice Selection from the Revelations, Translations, and Narrations of Joseph Smith, First Prophet, Seer, and Revelator to the Church of Jesus Christ of Latter-day Saints* (Liverpool: F. D. Richards, 1851), title page.

4. The 1851 *Pearl of Great Price* included the following items: the JST through Genesis 6:13 (now Selections from the Book of Moses), Matthew 23:39–24:51 from the JST (Joseph Smith—Matthew), the Book of Abraham, parts of five sections from the Doctrine and Covenants (no longer included), part of the Prophet's 1838 history (Joseph Smith—History), the Articles of Faith (not known by that title at the time), and a poem entitled "Truth" (now hymn 272 in the LDS hymnbook).

5. The name *foolscap* derived from paper in the eighteenth century that bore the watermark of a fool's cap.

Manuscript 1 (OT1).[6] The Book of Moses is found on the first twenty-one pages, in the handwriting of four different scribes:

Pages 1–10   Oliver Cowdery   Moses 1:1–5:43   June 1830–?

Pages 10–11   John Whitmer   Moses 5:43–6:18   Oct. 21, 1830; Nov. 30, 1830

Pages 11–14   Emma Smith   Moses 6:19–52   Dec. 1, 1830

Pages 14–15   John Whitmer   Moses 6:52–7:1   Dec. 1830

Pages 15–21   Sidney Rigdon   Moses 7:2–8:30   Dec. 1830; Feb. 1831

The work of the JST began either in Harmony, Pennsylvania; Colesville, New York; or Fayette, New York. It continued in Fayette and then in Kirtland, Ohio. The starting month, June 1830, is written on OT1, page 1. Oliver Cowdery, taking dictation from Joseph Smith, wrote the first ten pages. In October he left on the Lamanite Mission that introduced the restored gospel in Ohio and Missouri.[7] He was replaced as scribe by John Whitmer, who wrote the date October 21, 1830, on page 10 and started his first brief service as scribe. Farther down the same page, Whitmer inserted the date November 30, 1830, and wrote more. Emma Smith then wrote slightly more than two pages. She began by writing "Dec 1rst" at the bottom of page 11 and wrote to the top of page 14. The previous July, she had been called in a revelation to write for the Prophet when his regular scribe (at that time Oliver Cowdery) was unavailable (see D&C 25:6). Her work on the JST manuscript was in fulfilment of that calling. John Whitmer resumed scribing again and wrote on two more pages, after which Sidney Rigdon's handwriting first appears. Rigdon had

---

6. OT1 is housed in the Library-Archives of the Community of Christ in Independence, Missouri. In some older publications, this document is titled "Old Testament Manuscript 2," based on a misunderstanding by early archivists regarding the sequence of the New Translation.

7. See Joseph Smith, *The Papers of Joseph Smith: Vol. 1, Autobiographical and Historical Writings*, ed. Dean C. Jessee (Salt Lake City: Deseret Book, 1989), 324–25; D&C 28:8–10.

Old Testament Manuscript 1, page 10, showing the dates October 21, 1830,
and November 30, 1830; handwriting of Oliver Cowdery (lines 1–5)
and John Whitmer; Moses 5:41–6:2

Old Testament Manuscript 1, page 15, December 1830; handwriting of John Whitmer (to bracket on line 16) and Sidney Rigdon; Moses 6:64–7:10

arrived in Fayette on December 10, 1830, and soon thereafter was appointed by revelation to be Joseph Smith's scribe (see D&C 35:20). The translation was interrupted when the Prophet prepared to move from New York to Ohio in January 1831. He arrived in Kirtland, Ohio, on about the first of February and soon began anew his work on the New Translation, again with Sidney Rigdon as scribe. It was there that the Book of Moses was finished in February 1831. Rigdon continued as scribe for the rest of OT1, which ends in Genesis 24. He also wrote large portions of the other JST manuscripts, and more than half of the pages of the entire New Translation are in his handwriting.

In general, Joseph Smith's scribes wrote without using punctuation, which sometimes makes it difficult to interpret the intended meaning of his words. Some of the other JST manuscripts were punctuated heavily by later hands, but that is not the case with OT1.

By April 5, 1831, a duplicate of OT1 had been made, called Old Testament Manuscript 2 (OT2). Although it started as a copy of the dictated manuscript, OT2 later became the document on which the Prophet continued his translation to the end of the Old Testament. But additional corrections were also made on OT1. Sometime after Oliver Cowdery returned from the Lamanite Mission in summer 1831, Joseph Smith apparently dictated to him some revisions to what he had translated already. Oliver Cowdery recorded those changes on OT1.[8] But OT2 had been written prior to that date, and thus those changes were never recorded on the new manuscript. As a result, they were later overlooked, and they have never been put in place in the Book of Moses. Similarly, six small changes, apparently in the handwriting of Joseph Smith, were inserted in OT1 sometime after the original dictation.[9]

The text of OT1 is one of the most significant documents of the restored gospel. In its doctrinal contributions it is on par with the greatest of revelations. But OT1 is not the complete and final text of the Book of Moses, because that is found on OT2, on which Joseph Smith made further inspired corrections and additions.

---

8. See OT1, pages 11, 12, and 19.

9. See OT1, page 7.

Old Testament Manuscript 2

Old Testament Manuscript 2 (OT2) began as a transcription—a duplicate copy—of OT1.[10] It was created by John Whitmer, who was called in a
revelation of March 8, 1831, to assist Joseph Smith "in transcribing all
things which shall be given" to him (D&C 47:1). Whitmer probably began
copying OT1 shortly after the revelation was received. The date he finished
the work is written at the end of OT1: "April 5th 1831 transcribed thus
far."[11] The Book of Moses is found on the first twenty-seven pages of OT2,
and probably all of it was copied during the month of March 1831. That
same month, Joseph Smith interrupted his Old Testament translation at
Genesis 24 to work on the New Testament as he had been instructed in a
revelation (see D&C 45:60–61). When the New Testament was finished in
July 1832, he returned to finish the Old Testament. But when he did, he
used OT2 rather than OT1 as the working document. It was on OT2 that
he continued his translation to the end of Malachi, which he finished in
July 1833.[12] And it was on OT2 that he made additional revisions to the
work in Genesis that he had already translated. When it was completed,
OT2 was 119 pages long.

Unlike OT1, which was an original dictation and contains very few
later changes, OT2 shows signs of subsequent correcting, editing, and
emending. In the Book of Moses section (pages 1–27), some editing was
done to correct copying errors or errors made when the Prophet was dictating from his Bible and his eyes skipped from one line to the next, resulting
in omitted material. The manuscript shows that John Whitmer made corrections to his own copying, and Sidney Rigdon made corrections when he
compared the transcription to corresponding Bible passages.[13] OT2 contains
verse divisions and verse numbers that were inserted by Joseph Smith's

10. OT2 is housed in the Library-Archives of the Community of Christ in
    Independence, Missouri. In some older publications, it is titled "Old Testament
    Manuscript 3."

11. See OT1, page 61.

12. The end date of the Old Testament and thus of the entire Joseph Smith Translation
    is noted at the end of Malachi: "Finished on the 2d day of July 1833" (OT2, page
    119).

13. For example, OT2, page 8, lines 14 and 16; see also Genesis 3:2–5.

Genesis 1st Chapter

A Revelation given to Joseph the Seer, June, 1830.

1 The words of God which he spake unto Moses, at a time when Moses was caught up into an exceeding high mountain, & he saw God face to face, & he talked with him, & the glory of God was upon him; therefore he could endure his presence, & he spake unto him,

2 saying, Behold, I am the Lord God Almighty, & endless is my name, for I am without beginning of days or end of years, & is this not endless?

3 & behold, thou art my Son, wherefore, look, & I will shew thee the workmanship of mine hands, but not all, for my works are without end, & also my words, for they never cease; wherefore, no man can behold all my works except he behold all my glory, & no man can behold all my glory, & afterwards remain in the flesh on the earth; & I have a

4 work for thee, Moses my Son; & thou art in the similitude of mine only begotten, & mine only begotten is & shall be the Saviour, for he is full of grace & truth; but there is none other God beside me, & all things are present with me, for I know them all; & now behold,

5 this one thing I shew unto thee, Moses my Son, for thou art in the World, & now I shew it thee; And it came to pass that

6 Moses looked & beheld the world upon which he was created, & as Moses beheld the world & the ends thereof & all the children of men which are & which were created, of the same he greatly marvelled & wondered; & the presence of God withdrew from Moses, that his glory was not upon him; & Moses was left unto himself; & as he was left unto himself he fell unto the earth; And it came to pass that it was for the space of many hours before Moses did again receive his natural strength like unto man; & he said unto himself, Now for this once I know that man is nothing, which thing I never had supposed; But now mine own eyes have beheld God, but not

7 mine natural but my spiritual eyes, for mine natural eyes could not have beheld, for I should have withered & died in his presence; But his glory was upon me & I beheld his face, for I was transfigured before him; & now it being to pass

8 that when Moses had said these words, Behold, Satan came tempting him, saying, Moses, son of man, worship me. And it came to pass that Moses lifted up his eyes and looked upon Satan & said, Who art thou? for behold, I am a Son of God in the similitude of his only begotten; & where is thy glory that I should worship thee? for behold, I could not look upon God except his glory should come upon me & I was transfigured before him; But I can look upon thee in the natural man; is it not so, surely? blessed be the name of my God,

Old Testament Manuscript 2, page 1, copied from Old Testament Manuscript 1, page 1, March 1831; handwriting of John Whitmer, corrections by Sidney Rigdon; Moses 1:1–15

clerks, as well as punctuation and capitalization changes that were made by unknown hands.

The most important changes made after the original transcription were those that were inserted by Joseph Smith. Sometime after Genesis of OT2 was written, the Prophet revisited the manuscript to make further revisions. Some of those are editorial in nature and clarify and smooth out the words of the dictated text. But others are inspired additions and corrections that provide new insights or even change the meaning of what had been written before. Sidney Rigdon was the scribe for all but a very few of the corrections, recording the words dictated by the Prophet. We do not know when the additional corrections were made. As far as we know, Sidney Rigdon served as Joseph Smith's scribe only until fall 1833, and thus it is likely that the changes were made before then, perhaps even while the original dictation of other parts of the Bible was still under way.

OT2 is an extraordinarily important document, containing as it does Joseph Smith's text of the Book of Moses with his latest corrections. It alone is not sufficient, however. When John Whitmer transcribed from OT1 to OT2, he worked carefully and conscientiously. But he did not produce an error-free text. The manuscript shows that he made numerous word changes as he transcribed, averaging about four and one-half changes per page. Some of the changes were reversed in later editions, but many have persisted to the present. About two-thirds of Whitmer's word changes appear to have been made intentionally.

Whitmer made grammatical corrections, such as these examples:[14]

OT1:	These words *was* spoken (Moses 1:42)
OT2:	These words *were* spoken
OT1:	all things *has its* likeness (Moses 6:63)
OT2:	all things *have their* likeness
OT1:	there *was* no poor among them (Moses 7:18)
OT2:	there *were* no poor among them

---

14. In some examples cited below, spelling or punctuation or both have been standardized for clarification.

OT1:	Zion *hath* I blessed (Moses 7:20)
OT2:	Zion *have* I blessed

OT1:	the saints arose and *was* crowned (Moses 7:56)
OT2:	the saints arose and *were* crowned

In some changes, Whitmer altered what he apparently believed were errors in the original text, as these examples illustrate:

OT1:	thou art in similitude (Moses 1:6)
OT2:	thou art in *the* similitude

OT1:	I am with *you* even *to* the end of thy days (Moses 1:26)
OT2:	I am with *thee* even *unto* the end of thy days

OT1:	the *waters* (Moses 2:2, 6)
OT2:	the *water*

OT1:	which *bore* record of the Father and the Son (Moses 5:9)
OT2:	which *beareth* record of the Father and the Son

OT1:	in the likeness of God *made* he him (Moses 6:8)
OT2:	in the likeness of God *created* he him

OT1:	I will give thee utterance (Moses 6:32)
OT2:	*and* I will give thee utterance

OT1:	could not stand *before* his presence (Moses 6:47)
OT2:	could not stand *in* his presence

OT1:	out of the *depths* of the sea (Moses 7:14, twice)
OT2:	out of the *depth* of the sea

OT1:	Messiah (Moses 7:53, twice)
OT2:	*the* Messiah

In some cases, Whitmer made word changes that go well beyond what the Prophet dictated, as in these examples:

OT1:	if thou doest well *shalt thou not* be accepted? (Moses 5:23)
OT2:	if thou doest well *thou shalt* be accepted

OT1:   things which were not visible (Moses 6:36)

OT2:   things which were not visible *to the natural eye*

OT1:   millions of earths like this (Moses 7:30)

OT2:   millions of *such* earths like this

OT1:   Noah called upon *men* (Moses 8:20)

OT2:   Noah called upon *the children of men*

About a third of the differences between OT1 and Whitmer's copy of it on OT2 appear to be unintended transcribing errors, as in these examples:

OT1:   the immortality and *the* eternal life of man (Moses 1:39)

OT2:   the immortality and eternal life of man

OT1:   and *the* light was good (Moses 2:4)

OT2:   and *that* light was good

OT1:   he *thought* to destroy the world (Moses 4:6)

OT2:   he *sought* to destroy the world

OT1:   *by* the sweat of thy face (Moses 4:25)

OT2:   *in* the sweat of thy face

OT1:   I have forgiven thee thy *transgressions* (Moses 6:53)

OT2:   I have forgiven thee thy *transgression*

OT1:   *And* great *tribulations* (Moses 7:61)

OT2:   *A* great *tribulation*

OT1:   sweep the earth *as with* the flood (Moses 7:62)

OT2:   sweep the earth *as* the flood

OT1:   and ye shall receive the *gift of the Holy Ghost* (Moses 8:24)

OT2:   and ye shall receive the *Holy Ghost*

OT1:   and if you do not *do* this (Moses 8:24)

OT2:   and if you do not this

There are about one and one-half of these apparent scribal errors per manuscript page. While some of them were discovered and corrected by later editors, some are still in the Book of Moses today.

OT1 and OT2 are the original manuscripts of the Book of Moses. Of these, OT2 is the most significant, containing the final product of Joseph Smith's revealed text. Aside from the imperfections that it contains as a result of transcription errors and grammatical and spelling anomalies, OT2 is the text of the Book of Moses as Joseph Smith intended it and as he left it to the Church. As far as we know, the Prophet kept these original manuscripts in his possession throughout this life. He looked forward to the day in which the entire New Translation would be published,[15] and the manuscripts were among his private property when he died.

Early Manuscripts and Printings

During Joseph Smith's lifetime, parts of his New Translation of the Bible were copied by hand, and some copies may have circulated among interested Church members. Today we know of only a few early extant copies. The earliest was made by John Whitmer, probably in January 1831. It includes the first five chapters of Genesis (Moses 1:1–8:12), rather hastily copied from the first twenty pages of OT1.[16] Edward Partridge made a copy of OT1 in about February 1831 in Kirtland, Ohio, not long after Joseph Smith and his scribe Sidney Rigdon arrived there. The surviving pages of the Partridge manuscript contain only Genesis 5:19–9:12 (including Moses 6:21–8:30).[17]

The earliest printing of Book of Moses material took place in August 1832, when Moses 7 was printed in its entirety in the Church's Independence, Missouri, newspaper, *The Evening and the Morning Star* (*EMS*).[18] In March 1833, Moses 6:43–68 was printed in the same newspaper,[19] and

---

15. See Robert J. Matthews, "Joseph Smith's Efforts to Publish His Bible Translation," *Ensign*, January 1983, 57–64.

16. This manuscript was preserved by the family of David Whitmer and acquired by the Reorganized Church of Jesus Christ of Latter Day Saints in 1903. It is housed in the Library-Archives of the Community of Christ in Independence, Missouri, and is catalogued as Old Testament Manuscript 3. In some older publications it was called "Old Testament Manuscript 1."

17. The Edward Partridge manuscript is housed in the Church Archives, the Church of Jesus Christ of Latter-day Saints, Salt Lake City, Utah.

18. See *The Evening and the Morning Star* 1, no. 3 (August 1832): 2–3.

19. See *The Evening and the Morning Star* 1, no. 10 (March 1833): 1.

EXTRACT FROM THE PROPHECY OF ENOCH.

AND it came to pass that Enoch continued his speech saying, Behold our father Adam taught these things, and many have believed and become the sons of God, and many have believed not and have perished in their sins, and are looking forth with fear, in torment, for the fiery indignation of the wrath of God to be poured out upon them. And from that time forth Enoch began to prophesy, saying unto the people, That, as I was journeying and stood upon the place Mahujah, and I cried unto the Lord, there came a voice out of heaven, saying, Turn ye and get ye upon the mount Simeon. And it came to pass that I turned and went upon the mount, and as I stood upon the mount, I beheld the heavens open, and I was clothed upon with glory, and I saw the Lord; he stood before my face, and he talked with me, even as a man talketh one with an other face to face; and he saith unto me, Look, and I will shew unto thee the the world for the space of many generations. And it came to pass that I beheld in the valley of Shum, and lo, a great people which dwelt in tents, which were the people of Shum. And again the Lord said unto me, Look, and I looked towards the north, and I beheld the people of Canaan, which dwelt in tents. And the Lord said unto me, Prophesy, and I prophesied saying, Behold the people of Canaan, which are numerous, shall go forth in battle array against the people of Shum, and shall slay them that they shall utterly be destroyed; and the people of Canaan shall divide themselves in the land, and the land shall be barren and unfruitful, and none other people shall dwell there but the people of Canaan; for behold the Lord shall curse the land with much heat, and the barrenness thereof shall go forth forever: And there was a blackness come upon all the children of Canaan, that they were despised among all people. And it came to pass that the Lord said unto me, Look, and I looked and beheld the land of Sharon, and the land of Enoch, and the land of Omner, and the land of Heni, and the land of Shem, and the land of Haner, and the land of Hanannihah, and all the inhabitants thereof; and the Lord said unto me, Go to this people and say unto them, Repent, lest I shall come out and smite them with a curse, and they die. And he

unto Enoch, Behold these thy brethren; they are the workmanship of mine own hands, and I gave unto them their knowledge, in the day I created them; and in the garden of Eden gave I unto man his agency; and unto thy brethren have I said, and also, gave commandment, That they should love one another; and that they should choose me their father, but behold they are without affection; and they hate their own blood; and the fire of mine indignation is kindled against them; and in my hot displeasure will I send in the floods upon them, for my fierce anger is kindled against them: Behold I am God; Man of Holiness is my name, Man of council is my name; and Endless and Eternal is my name, also. Wherefore, I can stretch forth mine hands and hold all the creations which I have made; and mine eye can pierce them, also; and among all the workmanship of mine hand, there has not been so great wickedness, as among thy brethren, but behold their sins shall be upon the heads of their fathers: Satan shall be their father, and misery shall be their doom; and the whole heavens shall weep over them, even all the workmanship of mine hands: Wherefore, should not the heavens weep, seeing these shall suffer? But behold, these, which thine eyes are upon, shall perish in the floods; and behold I will shut them up; a prison have I prepared for them:— And that which I have chosen hath plead before my face: Wherefore he suffereth for their sins, inasmuch as they will repent in the day that my chosen shall return unto me; and until that day, they shall be in torment: wherefore, for this shall the heavens weep; yea, and all the workmanship of mine hands.

And it came to pass, that the Lord spake unto Enoch and told Enoch all the doings of the children of men; wherefore Enoch knew, and looked upon their wickedness, and their misery, and wept, and stretched forth his arms, and his heart swelled wide as eternity; and his bowels yearned; and all eternity shook. And Enoch saw Noah, also, and his family; that the posterity of all the sons of Noah should be saved with a temporal salvation: wherefore he saw that Noah built an Ark; and the Lord smiled upon it, and held it in his own hand; but upon the residue of the wicked came the floods and swallowed them up. And as Enoch saw thus, he had bitterness of soul, and wept over his brethren, and said unto the heavens, I will re-

Moses 5:1–16 and 8:13–30 appeared the following month.[20] When the
Lectures on Faith (LF) were printed in the Doctrine and Covenants in 1835,
some passages from the New Translation were used in the second lecture,
including several verses from Genesis.[21] All of those early publications of
Book of Moses material—both in *The Evening and the Morning Star* and in
the Lectures on Faith—were based on the text of OT1, as a careful comparison reveals. Thus they do not contain the Prophet's latest corrections and
insertions. Nothing more was printed from the Book of Moses until early
in 1843, when a chapter appeared in the Church's Nauvoo, Illinois, newspaper, the *Times and Seasons* (*TS*). In January of that year, an installment in
the serial publication of Joseph Smith's history included the full text of
Moses 1.[22] That text is unique among the early publications. It was not
based on OT1 but on a copy that someone had made, about a decade earlier, of OT2 prior to the insertion of Joseph Smith's corrections. Thus it includes some of the unique characteristics of John Whitmer's transcription.
Like the earlier publications from *The Evening and the Morning Star* and the
Lectures on Faith, this publication was not always carefully done and not
always identical to the text on the original manuscripts. In several places,
editors or typesetters changed words in these early printings, often for reasons that are not apparent now. Among other changes, the Lectures on
Faith remove the first-person voice from the Creation account and modern-
ize much of the language of the text. The archaic pronouns *thou* and *ye* are
modernized to "you." Following are some examples of divergences from the
original manuscripts:

OT2:	for this *once* I know (Moses 1:10)
TS:	for this *cause* I know
OT1:	*transfigured* before him (Moses 1:14)
TS:	*strengthened* before him

---

20. See *The Evening and the Morning Star* 1, no. 11 (April 1833): 1–2.

21. See "Lecture Second," *Doctrine and Covenants of the Church of the Latter Day Saints*
(Kirtland, OH: F. G. Williams and Co., 1835), 13–18. It contained the following
passages from the Book of Moses: Moses 2:26–29; 3:15–17, 19–20; 4:14–19, 22–25;
5:1, 4–9, 19–23, 32–40.

22. See "History of Joseph Smith," *Times and Seasons* 4, no. 5 (January 16, 1843): 71–73.

11 And out of the ground the Lord God formed every beast of the field, and every fowl of the air, and commanded that they should be brought unto Adam, to see what he would call them. * * * And whatever Adam called every living creature, that was the name thereof. And Adam gave names to all cattle, and to the fowl of the air, and to every beast of the field.

12 From the foregoing we learn man's situation at his first creation; the knowledge with which he was endowed, and the high and exalted station in which he was placed—lord, or governor of all things on earth, and at the same time enjoying communion and intercourse with his Maker, without a vail to separate between. We shall next proceed to examine the account given of his fall, and of his being driven out of the garden of Eden, and from the presence of the Lord.

13 Moses proceeds: And they [Adam and Eve] heard the voice of the Lord God as they were walking in the garden in the cool of the day, and Adam and his wife hid themselves from the presence of the Lord God among the trees of the garden. And the Lord God called unto Adam, and said unto him, Where are you going? And he said, I heard your voice in the garden, and I was afraid, because I beheld that I was naked, and I hid myself.

14 And the Lord God said unto Adam, Who told you that you were naked? Have you eaten of the tree whereof I told you that you should not eat? If so, you should surely die? And the man said, The woman whom you gave me, and commanded that she should remain with me, gave me of the fruit of the tree, and I did eat.

15 And the Lord God said unto the woman, What is this which you have done? And the woman said, The serpent beguiled me, and I did eat.

16 And again, the Lord said unto the woman, I will greatly multiply your sorrow, and your conception: in sorrow you shall bring forth children; and your desire shall be to your husband, and he shall rule over you.

17 And the Lord God said unto Adam, because you have hearkened unto the voice of your wife, and have eaten of the fruit of the tree of which I commanded you, saying, You shall not eat of it! cursed shall be the ground for your sake; in sorrow you shall eat of it all the days of your life. Thorns also, and thistles shall it bring forth to you: and you shall eat the herb of the field. By the sweat of your face shall you eat bread, until you shall return unto the ground —for you shall surely die—for out of it you were taken; for dust you were, and unto dust you shall return. This was immediately followed by the fulfillment of what we previously said: Man was driven, or sent out of Eden.

18 Two important items are shown from the former quotations: First, After man was created, he was not left without intelligence, or understanding, to wander in darkness, and spend an existence in ignorance and doubt—on the great and important point which effected his happiness,—as to the real fact by whom he was created, or unto whom he was amenable for his conduct. God conversed with him face to face: in his presence he was permitted to stand, and from his own mouth he was permitted to receive instruction—he heard his voice, walked before him, and gazed upon his glory—while intelligence burst upon his understanding, and enabled him to give names to the vast assemblage of his Maker's works.

19 Secondly, we have seen, that, though man did transgress, his transgression did not deprive him of the previous knowledge with which he was endowed, relative to the existence and glory of his Creator;

Lectures on Faith, Lecture 2, 1835 Doctrine and Covenants, pages 14–15, showing Joseph Smith Translation language in modernized form

dered! and the presence of God withdrew from Moses, that his glory was not upon Moses; and Moses was left unto himself. And as he was left unto himself he fell unto the earth, and it came to pass, that it was for the space of many hours before Moses did again receive his natural strength like unto man; and he saith unto himself, now, for this cause I know that man is nothing, which thing I never had supposed; but now mine eyes, mine own eyes, but not mine eyes, for mine eyes could not have beheld; for I should have withered and died in his presence; but his glory was upon me. And I beheld his face, for I was transfigured before him.

And it came to pass that when Moses had said these words, behold Satan came tempting him, saying: Moses, son of man, worship me. And it came to pass, that Moses looked upon Satan, and said who art thou? for behold I am a son of God, in the similitude of h's only begotten; and where is thy glory, that I should worship thee? for behold I could not look upon God, except his glory should come upon me, and I were strengthened before him: But I can look upon thee in the natural man: Is it not so surely? Blessed is the name of my God, for his spirit hath not altogether withdrawn from me, or else, where is thy glory? for it is darkness unto me; and I am judge between thee and God: for God said unto me, worship God, for him only shalt thou serve: Get thou hence, Satan; deceive me not, for God said unto me, thou art after the similitude of mine only begotten. And he also gave me commandments, when he called unto me out of the "burning bush," saying: call upon God in the name of mine only begotten, and worship me. And again Moses said, I will not cease to call upon God: I have these things to inquire of him, for his glory has been upon me: wherefore I can judge between him and thee. Depart hence, Satan.

And now when Moses had said these words, Satan cried with a loud voice, and went upon the earth, and commanded, saying: I am the only begotten, worship me. And it came to pass that Moses began to fear exceedingly; and as he began to fear he saw the bitterness of hell: nevertheless, calling upon God, he received strength; and he commanded, saying: Depart from me, Satan, for this one God only will I worship, which is the God of glory. And now Satan began to tremble, and the earth shook; and Moses received strength, and called upon God, saying, in the name of Jesus Christ, depart hence Satan. And it came to pass, that Satan cried with a loud voice, with weeping and gnashing of teeth, and departed hence, even from the presence of Moses, that he beheld him not.

And now of this thing Moses bore record, but because of wickedness it is not had among the children of men. And it came to pass that when Satan had departed from the presence of Moses, he lifted up his eyes unto heaven, being filled with the Holy Ghost, which beareth record of the Father and the Son; and calling on the name of God he beheld his glory again, for it was upon him, and he heard a voice, saying: Blessed art thou Moses, for I the Almighty have chosen thee; and thou shall be made stronger than many waters; for they shall obey thy command as if thou wert God: And lo, I am with thee, even unto the end of thy days: for thou shalt deliver my people from bondage, even Israel my chosen. And it came to pass as Moses' voice was still speaking, he cast his eyes, and behold the earth, yea, even all the face of it, there was not a particle of it which he did not behold, descrying it by the spirit of God.— And he beheld also the inhabitants thereof, and there was not a soul which he beheld not, and he discerned them by the spirit of God: And their numbers were great, even numberless as the sand upon the sea shore: And he beheld many lands; and each land was called earth, and there were inhabitants on the face thereof. And it came to pass that Moses called upon God, saying, tell me, I pray thee, why these things are so, and by what thou madest them? And behold the glory of God was upon Moses, so that Moses stood in the presence of God, and he talked with Moses, face to face; and the Lord God said unto Moses, for mine own purpose have I made these things. Here is wisdom, and it remaineth in me. And by the word of my power have I created them, which is mine only begotten Son, who is full of grace and truth: And worlds without number have I created; and I also created them for mine own purpose; and by the Son I created them, which is mine only begotten: And the first men, of all men, have I called Adam, which is many. But only an account of this earth, and the inhabitants thereof, give I unto you: For behold there are many worlds which have passed away by the words of my power. And there are many which now stand, and innumerable are they unto man; but all things are numbered unto me, for they are mine, and I know them.— And it came to pass, that Moses spake unto the Lord, saying, Be merciful unto thy servant, O God, and tell me concerning this earth, and the inhabitants thereof; and also the heavens, and then thy servant will be content. And the

"History of Joseph Smith," Times and Seasons, *January 16, 1843, page 72, Nauvoo, Illinois; Moses 1:8–37*

OT2:	and *wrent* upon the earth (Moses 1:19)
TS:	and *went* upon the earth
OT1, OT2:	departed hence, *yea* from the presence of Moses (Moses 1:22)
TS:	departed hence, *even* from the presence of Moses
OT1, OT2:	and *numberless* are they unto man (Moses 1:35)
TS:	and *innumerable* are they unto man
OT1:	and said unto him, *Where goest thou?* And he said, I heard *thy* voice (Moses 4:15–16)
LF:	and said unto him, *Where are you going?* And he said, I heard *your* voice
OT1, OT2:	and stood *in* the place Mahujah (Moses 7:2)
EMS:	and stood *upon* the place Mahujah
OT2:	the *powers* of Satan *were* upon all the face of the earth (Moses 7:24)
EMS:	the *power* of Satan *was* upon all the face of the earth
OT1, OT2:	*And* whoso cometh in at the gate (Moses 7:53)
EMS:	Whoso cometh in at the gate

After the Prophet's death, another significant manuscript copy was made. In summer 1845, John M. Bernhisel, a trusted friend of Joseph and Emma Smith, was given permission by the Prophet's widow to borrow the Joseph Smith Translation manuscripts and to study and copy them. While he had the documents in his possession, he made a copy that includes parts of the Old and New Testaments. The Old Testament material was copied from OT2. Although the Bernhisel manuscript is incomplete and not always an accurate reproduction of the original, it is an important document because it reflects the state of the New Translation shortly after Joseph Smith's death.[23]

---

23. For the Bernhisel manuscript, see Robert J. Matthews, *"A Plainer Translation": Joseph Smith's Translation of the Bible—A History and Commentary* (Provo, UT: Brigham Young University Press, 1975), 117–40. The manuscript is housed in the Church Archives, the Church of Jesus Christ of Latter-day Saints, Salt Lake City, Utah.

The 1851 *Pearl of Great Price*

In 1851 Elder Franklin D. Richards created what we now call the Book of Moses by publishing Genesis excerpts from the Joseph Smith Translation in his British Mission pamphlet, the *Pearl of Great Price.* His excerpts were presented in two parts at the beginning of the pamphlet. The first was "Extracts from the prophecy of Enoch, containing also a revelation of the gospel unto our father Adam, after he was driven out from the Garden of Eden." It included part of Moses 6 and all of Moses 7.[24] The second part was called "The words of God, which he spake unto Moses at the time when Moses was caught up into an exceeding high mountain, and he saw God face to face, and he talked with him, and the glory of God was upon Moses; therefore Moses could endure his presence." That section included all of chapters 1–3 and parts of chapters 4, 5, and 8.[25] Altogether, the 1851 *Pearl of Great Price* contained Moses 1:1–4:19, 22–25; 5:1–16, 19–23, 32–40; 6:43–7:69; 8:13–30. Not included were sizable portions of chapters 4, 5, 6, and 8. Most of the Book of Moses material in the 1851 *Pearl of Great Price* had been published years earlier in *The Evening and the Morning Star,* the Lectures on Faith, and the *Times and Seasons.* Those appear to have been sources that Elder Richards used for his publication. Yet some of the material had never been printed before. Because Elder Richards had no access to original documents, it follows that he must have had handwritten copies of earlier manuscripts that contributed as sources for parts of his publication. All of his printed sources were based on OT1, except for Moses 1, which was based on OT2 before it received the Prophet's later revisions, as noted above. His manuscript sources show affinities both to OT1 and to OT2 before it was finished. The passages included in the 1851 *Pearl of Great Price* were not copied with perfect accuracy, and changes were introduced into the text at a few places. Thus the 1851 Book of Moses was not always correctly transcribed, nor did it contain Joseph Smith's best text of the record of Moses.

At the same time the *Pearl of Great Price* was being prepared, Elder Richards published part of the Book of Moses material (Moses 2:1–4:13) in

---

24. Moses 6:43–7:69.

25. Moses 1:1–4:19, 22–25; 5:1–16, 19–23, 32–40; 8:13–30.

Pearl of Great Price.

EXTRACTS FROM THE PROPHECY OF ENOCH, CONTAINING ALSO A REVELATION OF THE GOSPEL UNTO OUR FATHER ADAM, AFTER HE WAS DRIVEN OUT FROM THE GARDEN OF EDEN.

Revealed to Joseph Smith, December, 1830

" AND Enoch continued his speech, saying, The Lord which spake with me, the same is the God of heaven, and He is my God, and your God, and ye are my brethren, and why counsel ye yourselves, and deny the God of heaven ?

The heavens hath he made: the earth is his footstool, and the foundation thereof is his: Behold he hath laid it, an host of men hath he brought in upon the face thereof. And death hath come upon our fathers: nevertheless we know them, and cannot deny, and even the first of all we know, even Adam. For a book of remembrance we have written among us, according to the pattern given by the finger of God: and it is given in our own language.

And as Enoch spake forth the words of God, the people trembled, and could not stand before his presence: and he said unto them, because that Adam fell we are: and by his fall came death; and we are made partakers of misery and woe. Behold Satan hath come among the children of men, and tempteth them to worship him: and men have become carnal, sensual, and devilish, and are shut out from the presence of God. But God hath made known unto my fathers, that all men must repent.

And he called upon our father Adam by his own voice, saying, I am God: I made the world, and men before they were. And he also said unto him, if thou wilt turn unto me, and hearken unto my voice, and believe, and repent of all thy transgressions, and be baptized even by water, in the name of mine Only Begotten Son, which is full of grace and truth, which is Jesus Christ, the only name which shall be given under heaven, whereby salvation shall come unto the children of men ; ye shall ask all things in His name, and whatever ye shall ask, it shall be given.

And our father Adam spake unto the Lord, and said, Why is it that men

B

"*Extracts from the Prophecy of Enoch,*" Pearl of Great Price, *1851, Liverpool, England, page 1; Moses 6:43–53*

the British Mission periodical, the *Millennial Star*, of which he was the editor.[26] That material is the same as the corresponding passages that were published a few months later in the *Pearl of Great Price*.

Despite its incompleteness and imperfections, the 1851 Book of Moses was a tremendous blessing for the Church. Very few Latter-day Saints then had access to the New Translation printings from the newspapers of the 1830s and 1840s. Elder Richards's *Pearl of Great Price* brought thousands of Latter-day Saints into contact with great revelations to Joseph Smith of which most Church members were entirely unaware. It introduced generations to an important part of the Restoration and developed in them a greater love for the Prophet and his work. It went far to fulfill the wish that Elder Richards expressed in his preface, that "sinners, as well as Saints, will know that JOSEPH SMITH was one of the greatest men that ever lived upon the earth, and that under God he was the Prophet and founder of the dispensation of the fulness of times, in which will be gathered together into one all things which are in Christ, both which are in heaven and which are on earth."[27]

The 1866–67 RLDS Committee Manuscript

At the April 1866 conference of the Reorganized Church of Jesus Christ of Latter Day Saints, the decision was made to publish Joseph Smith's New Translation of the Bible. In less than two years, the efforts of preparing the text, setting the type, stereotyping printing plates, and printing and binding the signatures bore fruit. In December 1867 the edited transcription of Joseph Smith's entire Bible revision was published in Bible format, titled *The Holy Scriptures*.[28] This publication is still in print today, with its most recent edition having come out in 1991. Since the nineteenth

---

26. See *The Latter-Day Saints' Millennial Star* 13, no. 6 (March 15, 1851): 90–93.

27. *The Pearl of Great Price*, 1851, vi.

28. *The Holy Scriptures, Translated and Corrected by the Spirit of Revelation. By Joseph Smith, Jr., the Seer.* (Plano, IL: The [Reorganized] Church of Jesus Christ of Latter-Day Saints, 1867). For convenience, I will refer to it as the "*Inspired Version*," even though it did not receive that title until later.

century, it has been popularly called the *Inspired Version*, a name that was added officially to the title page in 1936.[29]

To prepare the Bible publication, the original JST manuscripts were first obtained from Emma Smith Bidamon, the Prophet's widow, who had preserved them in her possession since Joseph Smith's death in 1844. In order to protect the original manuscripts and facilitate the publication, church leaders determined that a printer's copy would be transcribed. At the April conference it was resolved "That the Manuscript of the Scriptures, be engrossed, and the engrossed copy be put into the hands of the printer, with a view to the preservation of the original copy."[30] To *engross* means to make a copy, in this case a copy that could be edited and prepared for publication. Marietta H. Faulconer and Mark H. Forscutt were employed to make the transcription. Faulconer copied the text from Genesis 1 through Psalms; Forscutt finished the work to the end of the New Testament. The manuscript they produced is called the Committee Manuscript (CM).[31] The Book of Moses material is found on its first fifty-nine pages, transcribed by Marietta Faulconer.[32]

When one examines the RLDS Committee Manuscript carefully, one can determine the history of its preparation. That history has heretofore not been well understood, but it is important for Latter-day Saints because today's Book of Moses—indeed, every edition of the Book of Moses since 1878—uses the text that was established in the 1866–67 RLDS Committee Manuscript, with some variations. The writing on the manuscript reveals that the document was produced in three stages.

First, Marietta Faulconer began the Committee Manuscript by transcribing OT1, assuming incorrectly that it was the document that contained the

---

29. The story of the preparation and publication of the 1867 *Inspired Version* is summarized in Matthews, *"A Plainer Translation,"* 141–69, and in Richard P. Howard, *Restoration Scriptures: A Study of Their Textual Development*, rev. and enl. (Independence, MO: Herald, 1995), 111–18.

30. *The True Latter Day Saints' Herald* 9, no. 8 (April 15, 1866): 125.

31. The 1866–67 Committee Manuscript is housed in the Library-Archives, Community of Christ, Independence, Missouri.

32. The first few pages of the manuscript are in the handwriting of Joseph Smith III, who apparently recopied them after editing Faulconer's manuscript pages.

Prophet's intended text. It is evident that at that time she, and perhaps RLDS officials as well, did not understand that OT1 had been superceded by the later manuscript OT2, on which Joseph Smith had made additional corrections. OT1 lacked not only the grammatical and literary refinements that the Prophet had inserted into the text, but it also lacked his later content changes, rewordings, and additions. It is clear that Faulconer's intent was to copy faithfully from the original without editing, except to correct spelling. For the most part she succeeded, even reproducing obvious grammatical errors. But at the same time, her eyes frequently skipped words on the page, omitting text. Either consciously or accidentally, she also made a few small word changes, as these examples show:

OT1:	by the sweat of *the* brow (Moses 5:1)
CM:	by the sweat of *his* brow
OT1:	And in *these* days (Moses 6:15)
CM:	And in *those* days
OT1:	there was a blackness *come* (Moses 7:8)
CM:	there was a blackness *came*
OT1:	and all the *creation* of God mourned (Moses 7:56)
CM:	and all the *creations* of God mourned

The positive result of Faulconer's decision to copy OT1 was that she did not copy onto the Committee Manuscript the scribal errors and anomalies that John Whitmer had added in OT2.

In the second stage of the preparation of the Committee Manuscript, Joseph Smith III proofed and corrected Faulconer's transcription against OT2. The Prophet's son and president of the RLDS Church was the chair of the committee that oversaw the publication of the *Inspired Version*. In his autobiography he reports that he went through Faulconer's transcription and edited it before sending it on to its production.[33] The Committee Manuscript itself attests to his work, showing his handwriting in many places. Because Faulconer's eyes had skipped text so frequently, President Smith's edit was indispensable. It is clear that he realized that Faulconer had copied

---

33. See Mary Audentia Smith Anderson, ed., "The Memoirs of President Joseph Smith (1832–1914)," *Saints' Herald* 82, no. 26 (June 25, 1935): 818.

the wrong text, but rather than discarding her transcription and starting a new one from the proper original, he decided to correct her writing on the manuscript by editing it against OT2. He changed words to match those in OT2 and added the insertions between the lines as they appeared on OT2. In doing so he restored his father's corrections to the text. Unfortunately, this process deleted the corrections that the Prophet had made to OT1 that were never transcribed onto OT2. Joseph Smith III deleted those OT1 insertions and replaced them with the uncorrected text from OT2. As a result, they were not included in the *Inspired Version,* and they have never been in the Pearl of Great Price. President Smith's work was done very carefully and very accurately, but while he restored the passages that Faulconer had inadvertently omitted, he also copied onto the Committee Manuscript some of the errors that John Whitmer had made in OT2. And he also made a very few small transcription errors of his own, including this one:

OT2:   coats of *skin* (Moses 4:27)

CM: coats of *skins*

Because Joseph Smith III was preparing the text for publication, in a few places he corrected grammatical problems, as these examples show:[34]

OT2:   he had *drew* away many after him (Moses 4:6)
CM: he had *drawn* away many after him

OT2:   were it not for our transgression we *should never had* seed, and *should never had known* good and evil (Moses 5:11)
CM: were it not for our transgression, we *never should have had* seed, and *never should have known* good and evil

OT2:   saying unto the tent keepers, tarry *thou* here (Moses 6:38)
CM: saying unto the tent keepers, tarry *ye* here

OT2:   no man laid *their* hands on him (Moses 6:39)
CM: no man laid hands on him

---

34. Probably for the same reasons, the 1851 *Pearl of Great Price* had already made the same grammatical corrections in Moses 4:6 and 5:11.

In some places he edited the wording apparently to correct the style:

OT2:	and his wife and many of his brethren *and* dwelt (Moses 5:41)
CM:	and *with* his wife and many of his brethren dwelt
OT2:	even him *who* he declared should come (Moses 5:57)
CM:	even him *whom* he declared should come
OT2:	they were of one heart, and *of* one mind (Moses 7:18)
CM:	they were of one heart, and one mind
OT2:	how is it the heavens weep (Moses 7:28)
CM:	how is it *that* the heavens weep

The third stage in the production of the Committee Manuscript text is also in evidence on the pages. After Joseph Smith III had corrected Faulconer's transcription to make it consistent with the Prophet's final text, he returned to the Committee Manuscript and deleted many of Joseph Smith's corrections. The manuscript shows that he lined out many of the insertions that Joseph Smith had dictated to his scribes and replaced them with the earlier readings. This happened especially in chapters 1 and 7. In those chapters, the general rule seems to be that he left his father's changes that corrected the grammar or clarified the wording but deleted those that changed the meaning of the text or added new insights. The consequence was that his editing reverted many OT2 readings back to those found in OT1, thereby overruling much of his father's work on the text. Many examples can be shown of Joseph Smith's corrections, large and small, that were excluded in this way from the 1867 *Inspired Version* and thus never have been included in the Pearl of Great Price. The following OT2 passages represent Joseph Smith's text, and the CM passages show what was finalized on the Committee Manuscript and passed on in the *Inspired Version* and the Book of Moses:

OT2:	*But* Moses *lifted up his eyes and* looked upon Satan (Moses 1:13)
CM:	*And it came to pass that* Moses looked upon Satan
OT2:	they shall obey thy command even as *my commandments* (Moses 1:25)
CM:	they shall obey thy command even as *if thou wert God*

OT2:   called upon God, saying, *Show* me . . . and by *whom* thou madest them (Moses 1:30)

CM: called upon God, saying, *Tell* me . . . and by *what* thou madest them

OT2:   And the Lord God spake unto Moses *of the heavens, saying, These* are many (Moses 1:37)

CM: And the Lord God spake unto Moses, *saying, The heavens, there* are many

OT2:   the record of heaven, the Comforter, the *keys of the kingdom of heaven* (Moses 6:61)

CM: the record of heaven, the Comforter, the *peaceable things of immortal glory*

OT2:   he had a great chain in his hand, and *he* veiled the whole face of the earth (Moses 7:26)

CM: he had a great chain in his hand, and *it* veiled the whole face of the earth

OT2:   *Enoch* looked upon the residue of the people and wept. *And he beheld and lo, the heavens wept also* and shed forth their tears (Moses 7:28)

CM: *the God of heaven* looked upon the residue of the people, and wept; and *Enoch bore record of it, saying, How is it that the heavens weep* and shed forth their tears . . . ?

OT2:   and thy *presence* is there (Moses 7:30)
CM: and thy *bosom* is there

OT2:   I gave unto them their *intelligence* (Moses 7:32)
CM: I gave unto them their *knowledge in the day that I created them*

OT2:   And in the Garden of Eden, *man had* agency (Moses 7:32)

CM: And in the Garden of Eden, *gave I unto man his* agency

OT2:   and that they should *serve me their God* (Moses 7:33)
CM: and that they should *choose me their Father*

48

face and have no end. How is it that thou canst weep? The Lord said unto Enoch, Behold, these thy brethren; they are the workmanship of mine own hands, and I gave unto them their knowledge in the day I created them; and in the Garden of Eden, gave I unto man his agency; And unto thy brethren have I said, and also gave commandment, that they should love one another; And that they should choose me their Father; but, behold, they are without affection, and they hate their own blood; And the fire of mine indignation is kindled against them; And in my hot displeasure will I send in the floods upon them; for my fierce anger is kindled against them. Behold, I am God; Man of Holiness is my name; Man of Council is my name; And Endless, & Eternal is my name, also. Wherefore, I can stretch forth my hands and hold all the creations which I have made, And mine eye can pierce them also. And among all the workmanship of my hands there has not been so great wickedness, as among thy brethren; But, behold, their sins shall be upon the heads of their fathers; Satan shall be their father, and

Committee Manuscript, Reorganized Church of Jesus Christ of Latter Day Saints, 1866–67, page 48; handwriting of Marietta H. Faulconer, corrections by Joseph Smith III; Moses 7:31–37

OT2:   Satan shall be their *master* (Moses 7:37)

CM: Satan shall be their *father*

OT2:   And *he whom* I have chosen (Moses 7:39)

CM: And *that which* I have chosen

OT2:   stretched forth his arms, and *he beheld* eternity (Moses 7:41)

CM: stretched forth his arms, and *his heart swelled wide as* eternity

OT2:   in the name of thine Only Begotten (Moses 7:50)

CM: in the name of thine Only Begotten, *even Jesus Christ*

OT2:   that *from* a remnant of his seed should *come* all nations (Moses 7:52)

CM: that a remnant of his seed should *always be found among* all nations

When one compares the editing on the RLDS Committee Manuscript with the earliest publications of New Translation material, one can see the origin of the changes that Joseph Smith III made. After preparing the Committee Manuscript to match OT2, he decided to check it against the texts as they were published in *The Evening and the Morning Star* in 1832–33 and the *Times and Seasons* in 1843. His revisions on the manuscript proof it against those publications and change its words to match theirs. One evidence for this is the fact that idiosyncratic readings in those newspapers that are not based either on OT1 or on OT2 are inserted and reproduced faithfully in the Committee Manuscript, as in these examples:

OT1:   in the natural man, *if not so surely* blessed *be* (Moses 1:14–15)

OT2:   in the natural man! *surely* blessed *be*

TS, CM: in the natural man: *Is it not so surely?* Blessed *is*

OT1, OT2:   for it is *blackness* unto me (Moses 1:15)

TS, CM: for it is *darkness* unto me

OT1, OT2:   and by the *same* I created them (Moses 1:33)

TS, CM: and by the *Son* I created them

OT1, OT2:   And Enoch said unto the *heavens* (Moses 7:29)

EMS, CM: And Enoch said unto the *Lord*

Why Joseph Smith III made these changes in the New Translation text is not known. He apparently felt that the chapters as published in *The Evening and the Morning Star* and the *Times and Seasons* were superior to what was written on OT2. This misunderstanding is very significant. Not only does the printed *Inspired Version* not reflect accurately the text of Genesis as Joseph Smith prepared it, but the same is also true of every edition of the Book of Moses since 1878, because the 1878 Book of Moses was taken directly from the 1867 *Inspired Version*.

Joseph Smith's scribes used inconsistent capitalization and very little punctuation as they wrote. Unidentified hands inserted punctuation and corrected capitalization in OT2, but we do not know when those processes took place. The verse numbers in OT2 were inserted by the Prophet's scribes or clerks.[35] The punctuation on the Committee Manuscript appears to have been inserted after the transcription. It tends to be rather heavy and often obscures the flow of the text. The Committee Manuscript's verse divisions were added after the transcription as well. They rarely follow those that were inserted in OT2 by Joseph Smith's assistants.

On the OT2 manuscript, a very few isolated words are written, usually in pencil, that are not in the handwriting of Joseph Smith's known scribes. The insertions identify obvious grammatical errors[36] or errors made in the transcription process that others did not notice.[37] They appear to have been written by Joseph Smith III, who perhaps penciled them in while he was working on the Committee Manuscript in 1867 or later.

---

35. The OT2 verse divisions are evident in the Bernhisel Manuscript, which was copied from OT2 in the summer of 1845. The evidence for punctuation and capitalization is less clear. Bernhisel did not include the OT2 punctuation or capitalization insertions, so perhaps they were not yet on the manuscript. But he also did not capitalize all the words that the original scribes capitalized, and he may have simply ignored all but verse-ending punctuation.

36. For example, OT2, page 16, line 7 from bottom ("ye").

37. For example, OT2, page 23, lines 13 ("looked") and 28 ("filthiness").

The 1867 *Inspired Version*

The 1867 *Inspired Version* (*IV*) is an edited, printed transcription of the entire Joseph Smith Translation of the Bible. It was typeset not from Joseph Smith's original manuscripts but from the RLDS Committee Manuscript. Joseph Smith III oversaw the project and took it seriously as a sacred duty.[38]

In the Book of Moses material in the *Inspired Version* ("A Revelation, Given to Joseph the Seer, June, A.D. 1830" and Genesis 1:1–8:18), the text differs in some instances from what was written on the Committee Manuscript. It is impossible to tell whether the changes were made by the typesetters or by the publication committee in proofs. Some of the changes appear to be the result of conscious editing, for reasons that are not always clear, but some changes are probably accidental. Following are examples of changes:

OT2:	in the name of *his Son* (Moses 1:21)
CM:	in the name of *Jesus Christ*
IV:	in the name of *the Only Begotten*
OT1, OT2, CM:	in the day *that* thou eatest thereof (Moses 3:17)
IV:	in the day thou eatest thereof
OT1, OT2, CM:	gave unto them *commandment* (Moses 5:5)
IV:	gave unto them *commandments*
OT1, CM:	I have forgiven thee thy *transgressions* in the Garden of Eden (Moses 6:53)
IV:	I have forgiven thee thy *transgression* in the Garden of Eden
OT1, OT2, CM:	that ye *may* be sanctified from all sin (Moses 6:59)
IV:	that ye *might* be sanctified from all sin
OT2, CM:	and there *were* no poor among them (Moses 7:18)
IV:	and there *was* no poor among them

---

38. See "Memoirs of President Joseph Smith," 818.

THE

HOLY SCRIPTURES,

TRANSLATED AND CORRECTED

BY THE

SPIRIT OF REVELATION,

BY

JOSEPH SMITH, Jr.,

THE SEER.

PUBLISHED BY THE
CHURCH OF JESUS CHRIST OF LATTER-DAY SAINTS.

PLANO, ILL.:
JOSEPH SMITH, I. L. ROGERS, E. ROBINSON,
PUBLISHING COMMITTEE.
1867.

Title page, 1867 Inspired Version, *Plano, Illinois*

A REVELATION, GIVEN TO JOSEPH THE SEER,

JUNE, A. D. 1830.

THE words of God which he spake unto Moses, at a time when Moses was caught up into an exceeding high mountain, and he saw God face to face, and he talked with him, and the glory of God was upon Moses; therefore Moses could endure his presence.

2 And God spake unto Moses, saying, Behold, I am the Lord God Almighty, and endless is my name, for I am without beginning of days or end of years; and is not this endless?

3 And behold, thou art my son, wherefore look, and I will show thee the workmanship of mine hands, but not all; for my works are without end, and also my words, for they never cease; wherefore, no man can behold all my works except he behold all my glory; and no man can behold all my glory, and afterwards remain in the flesh, on the earth.

4 And I have a work for thee, Moses, my son; and thou art in the similitude of mine Only Begotten; and my Only Begotten is and shall be the Saviour, for he is full of grace and truth; but there is no God beside me; and all things are present with me, for I know them all.

5 And now, behold, this one thing I show unto thee, Moses, my son; for thou art in the world, and now I show it unto thee.

6 And it came to pass, that Moses looked and beheld the world upon which he was created. And as Moses beheld the world, and the ends thereof, and all the children of men, which are and which were created; of the same he greatly marvelled, and wondered. And the presence of God withdrew from Moses, that his glory was not upon Moses; and Moses was left unto himself; and as he was left unto himself, he fell unto the earth.

7 And it came to pass, that it was for the space of many hours before Moses did again receive his natural strength like unto man; and he said unto himself, Now, for this cause, I know that man is nothing, which thing I never had supposed; but now mine eyes have beheld God; but not mine natural but my spiritual eyes, for mine natural eyes could not have beheld, for I should have withered and died in his presence; but his glory was upon me, and I beheld his face, for I was transfigured before him.

8 And now it came to pass, that when Moses had said these words, behold, Satan came tempting him, saying, Moses, son of man, worship me. And it came to pass that Moses looked upon Satan, and said, Who art thou, for behold I am a son of God, in the similitude of his Only Begotten; and where is thy glory, that I should worship thee? For, behold, I could not look upon God except his glory should come upon me, and I were transfigured before him. But I can look upon thee in the natural man. Is it not so surely?

9 Blessed be the name of my God, for his Spirit hath not altogether withdrawn from me; or else where is thy glory, for it is darkness unto me, and I can judge between thee and God; for God said unto me, Worship God, for him only shalt thou serve. Get thee hence, Satan, deceive me not; for God said unto me, Thou art after the similitude of mine Only Begotten.

10 And he also gave unto me commandment, when he called unto me out of the burning bush, saying, Call upon God in the name of mine Only Begotten, and worship me.

7

"A Revelation, Given to Joseph the Seer, June, A.D. 1830,"
1867 Inspired Version, page 7; Moses 1:1–17

THE

HOLY SCRIPTURES.

GENESIS.

CHAPTER I.

History of the creation.

AND it came to pass, that the Lord spake unto Moses, saying, Behold, I reveal unto you concerning this heaven and this earth; write the words which I speak.

2 I am the Beginning and the End; the Almighty God. By mine Only Begotten I created these things.

3 Yea, in the beginning I created the heaven, and the earth upon which thou standest.

4 And the earth was without form, and void; and I caused darkness to come up upon the face of the deep.

5 And my Spirit moved upon the face of the water, for I am God.

6 And I, God, said, Let there be light, and there was light.

7 And I, God, saw the light, and that light was good. And I, God, divided the light from the darkness.

8 And I, God, called the light day, and the darkness I called night. And this I did by the word of my power; and it was done as I spake. And the evening and the morning were the first day.

9 And again, I, God, said, Let there be a firmament in the midst of the water; and it was so, even as I spake. And I said, Let it divide the waters from the waters; and it was done.

10 And I, God, made the firmament, and divided the waters; yea, the great waters under the firmament, from the waters which were above the firmament; and it was so, even as I spake.

11 And I, God, called the firmament heaven. And the evening and the morning were the second day.

12 And I, God, said, Let the waters under the heaven be gathered together unto one place; and it was so. And I, God, said, Let there be dry land; and it was so.

13 And I, God, called the dry land earth; and the gathering together of the waters called I the sea.

14 And I, God, saw that all things which I had made were good.

15 And I, God, said, Let the earth bring forth grass; the herb yielding seed; the fruit tree yielding fruit after his kind; and the tree yielding fruit, whose seed should be in itself, upon the earth; and it was so, even as I spake.

16 And the earth brought forth grass; every herb yielding seed after his kind; and the tree yielding fruit, whose seed should be in itself, after his kind.

17 And I, God, saw that all things which I had made were good. And the evening and morning were the third day.

18 And I, God, said, Let there be lights in the firmament of the heaven, to divide the day from the night; and let them be for signs and for seasons, and for days and for years; and let them be for lights in the firmament of the heaven, to give light upon the earth; and it was so.

19 And I, God, made two great lights; the greater light to rule the day, and the lesser light to rule the night; and the greater light was the sun, and the lesser light was the moon.

20 And the stars also were made, even according to my word; and I, God, set them in the firmament of heaven, to give light upon the earth; and the sun to rule over the day, and the moon to rule over the night, and to divide the light from the darkness.

21 And I, God, saw that all things which I had made were good. And the evening and the morning were the fourth day.

22 And I, God, said, Let the waters bring forth abundantly, the moving

11

The 1867 *Inspired Version* was stereotyped—cast on metal plates that could be used to reprint the book almost indefinitely. The 1867 plates continued to be used until a new printing in 1936, which apparently was the 1867 text unchanged but in an enlarged format. That printing was the first to incorporate officially the name *Inspired Version.* The first new edition of the text since 1867 was the "New Corrected Edition" of 1944. Its text was checked against the early manuscripts, providing a more accurate transcription than its predecessor, with corrections in over three hundred verses.[39] A subsequent new edition appeared in 1991. It contains some small corrections,[40] but its most interesting feature for Latter-day Saints is its removal of Moses 1. Since 1867, "A Revelation, Given to Joseph the Seer, June, A.D. 1830" (Moses 1) had been included in the *Inspired Version* as a separate document before Genesis 1. Since 1864 it had also been published in the RLDS Doctrine and Covenants as section 22.[41] As it was available there, in 1991 it was dropped from the *Inspired Version.*[42]

The 1878 Pearl of Great Price

Desiring to make universally available the important revelations that were contained in Elder Richards's 1851 Liverpool *Pearl of Great Price*, LDS Church leaders decided to prepare a Churchwide publication of it, which appeared in 1878. The selections included in the new edition were for the most part the same as those in the 1851 edition. The Book of Moses continued in its place at the beginning of the book, but now in a significantly different form. The new Pearl of Great Price was prepared under the direction of Elder Orson Pratt of the Quorum of the Twelve Apostles. It appears

---

39. See Matthews, *"A Plainer Translation,"* 167–205. Matthews identified 352 verses in the 1944 edition that differ from the 1867 edition; Matthews, *"A Plainer Translation,"* 173, 179–89, 427–34. See also Howard, *Restoration Scriptures*, 119–27.

40. "Minor errors, mainly involving typography and punctuation." 1991 *Inspired Version*, "Foreword to the 1991 Edition," [6].

41. See Howard, *Restoration Scriptures,* 172, 177 n. 24.

42. "Because of space considerations only, it is not reprinted here." 1991 *Inspired Version*, "Foreword to the 1991 Edition," [7].

that he was aware that the 1851 Book of Moses had not been printed from Joseph Smith's final text of the New Translation, because Elder Pratt removed that text entirely and set in its place a better text of roughly the same material. Without the benefit of the original manuscripts (OT1 and OT2), he nonetheless knew that the RLDS *Inspired Version* contained a superior text, so he copied the Book of Moses material from that source and placed it into the new Pearl of Great Price. A careful comparison of the 1867 *Inspired Version* and the 1878 Book of Moses shows that the *Inspired Version* was the source for Elder Pratt's revised publication, and for the most part it was reproduced very carefully and faithfully. The punctuation, however, is generally simplified from that of the *Inspired Version*. The 1851 Book of Moses had been published in a fragmentary form, probably because Elder Richards only had fragments of the New Translation available to him. Nor was the 1851 edition in chronological order, because chapters 6 and 7 preceded chapters 1–3, which were followed by parts of chapters 4, 5, and 8. Only chapters 1–3 and 7 were complete, while the other chapters were presented only in part. Elder Pratt's 1878 Book of Moses presents the text in the contiguous form in which it appears on the original manuscripts. It comes from "A Revelation, Given to Joseph the Seer, June, A.D. 1830" (Moses 1) and Genesis 1:1–8:18 (Moses 2–8), the beginning nineteen pages of the printed *Inspired Version*,[43] corresponding to pages 1–21 of OT1 and 1–27 of OT2. The new Book of Moses text was divided into two chapters: "Visions of Moses" (Moses 1) and "Writings of Moses" (Moses 2–8).

The 1878 Book of Moses differs from the equivalent text in the *Inspired Version* in only a few places. Some of the changes appear to come from intentional editorial decisions:

OT1, OT2:	and *wrent* upon the earth (Moses 1:19)
IV:	and *went* upon the earth
1878:	and *rent* upon the earth

| OT1, OT2, *IV*: | who told thee *that* thou wast naked (Moses 4:17) |
| 1878: | who told thee thou wast naked |

---

43. Pages 7–9, 11–26.

WRITINGS OF MOSES,

AS REVEALED TO JOSEPH, THE SEER, IN DECEMBER, 1830.

And it came to pass that the Lord spake unto Moses, saying, Behold, I reveal unto you concerning this Heaven, and this Earth; write the words which I speak. I am the Beginning and the End, the Almighty God; by mine Only Begotten I created these things; yea, in the beginning I created the heaven, and the earth upon which thou standest. And the earth was without form, and void; and I caused darkness to come up upon the face of the deep; and my Spirit moved upon the face of the water; for I am God. And I, God, said Let there be light, and there was light; and I, God, saw the light, and that light was good. And I, God, divided the light from the darkness: and I, God, called the light, Day; and the darkness, I called Night; and this I did by the word of my power, and it was done as I spake; and the evening and the morning were the first day.

And again, I, God, said, Let there be a firmament in the midst of the water, and it was so, even as I spake; and I said, Let it divide the waters from the waters, and it was done; and I, God, made the firmament and divided the waters, yea, the great waters under the firmament, from the waters which were above the firmament, and it was so even as I spake, and I, God, called the firmament Heaven; and the evening and the morning were the second day.

And I, God, said, Let the waters under the heaven be gathered together unto one place, and it was so; and I, God, said, Let there be dry land, and it was so; and I, God, called the dry land, Earth; and the gathering together of the waters, called I the Sea; and I, God, saw that all things which I had made were good. And I, God, said, Let the earth bring forth grass, the herb yielding seed, the fruit tree yielding fruit, after his kind, and the tree yielding fruit, whose seed should be in itself upon the earth, and it was so even as I spake; and the earth brought forth grass, every herb yielding seed after his kind, and the tree yielding fruit, whose seed should be in itself, after his kind; and I, God, saw that all things which I had made were good; and the evening and the morning were the third day.

And I, God, said, Let there be lights in the firmament of the heaven, to divide the day from the night, and let them be for signs, and for seasons,

"Writings of Moses," 1878 Pearl of Great Price, page 4; Moses 2:1–14

OT1, *IV*:   and *commanded* that she should remain with me (Moses 4:18)

1878:   and *commandedst* that she should remain with me

OT1, OT2, *IV*:   see thou *show* them unto no man . . . except *they* that believe (Moses 4:32)

1878:   see thou *showest* them unto no man . . . except *to them* that believe

OT2, *IV*:   *and hosts* of men hath he brought in (Moses 6:44)

1878:   *an host* of men hath he brought in

OT1, OT2, *IV*:   marrying and *given* in marriage (Moses 8:21)

1878:   marrying and *giving* in marriage

OT1, OT2, *IV*:   the wickedness of *man* had become great (Moses 8:22)

1878:   the wickedness of *men* had become great

At least one example is most certainly an accident:

IV: ye *shall* not surely die (Moses 4:10)

1878:   ye *shalt* not surely die

And it is not clear whether the following example was intended or not:

OT1, OT2:   man of *council* is my name (Moses 7:35)

IV: Man of *Council* is my name

1878:   Man of *Counsel* is my name

In the October 1880 general conference of the Church of Jesus Christ of Latter-day Saints, the new Pearl of Great Price was presented for a sustaining vote and was accepted as scripture.[44] Since then it has been accounted as one of the standard works of the Church, and its remarkable contributions to our faith have been properly acknowledged.

Early Printings of the Pearl of Great Price

The 1878 edition of the Pearl of Great Price brought the newest standard work of the Church into mainstream Latter-day Saint culture and religious discourse. The Pearl of Great Price has been in print ever since then,

---

44. See *Deseret Evening News*, October 11, 1880, 2.

and early printings made it immediately inexpensive. In 1879, a year after the new edition came out, the Pearl of Great Price was typeset anew from the 1878 text and printed in Liverpool. The same plates were used again for Liverpool (1882) and Utah (1891) reprints. But the 1879 Book of Moses was not a perfect copy, as these two examples show:[45]

OT1, OT2, 1878:   for these many generations, *even* since the day that I created them (Moses 6:28)

1879:   for these many generations, *ever* since the day that I created them

OT1, OT2, 1878:   to gather out mine *own* elect (Moses 7:62)

1879:   to gather out mine elect

An 1888 printing by the Deseret News Company, Salt Lake City, was probably not intended to be a new edition but a new typesetting from the text of the 1878 edition. Even so, its Book of Moses is different in over twenty passages from the 1878 edition, with changes that resulted both from typesetting errors and from apparent editorial decisions. Among the changes that may have been intentional are the following:

OT1, OT2, 1878:   there are many worlds *which* have passed away (Moses 1:35)

1888:   there are many worlds *that* have passed away

OT1, OT2, 1878:   the firmament of *the* heaven (Moses 2:14, 17)

1888:   the firmament of heaven

OT1, OT2, 1878:   the fourth river was Euphrates (Moses 3:14)

1888:   the fourth river was *the* Euphrates

OT1, OT2, 1878:   did eat and *gave also* unto her husband (Moses 4:12)

1888:   did eat and *also gave* unto her husband

OT1, OT2, 1878:   *And* all the days of Seth were (Moses 6:16)

1888:   All the days of Seth were

---

45.   Both of these changes would later be adopted into the 1902 Pearl of Great Price.

Changes that appear to be accidental include these:

OT1, OT2, 1878: and a vagabond *shalt* thou be (Moses 5:37)
1888:   and a vagabond *shall* thou be

OT1, OT2, 1878: his offering thou didst *accept* (Moses 5:38)
1888:   his offering thou didst *except*

OT1, OT2, 1878: so will I come in the last days, *in the days* of
                 wickedness (Moses 7:60)
1888:   so will I come in the last days of wickedness

In some cases it is not clear whether a change was intentional, as these examples illustrate:

OT1, OT2, 1878: the evening and *the* morning were the second day
                 (Moses 2:8)
1888:   the evening and morning were the second day

OT2, 1878:   sware unto him *with* an oath (Moses 7:51)
1888:   sware unto him an oath

OT1, OT2, 1878: mighty men which are like unto *them* of old
                 (Moses 8:21)
1888:   mighty men which are like unto *men* of old

The 1888 printing of the Book of Moses would be of limited interest historically were it not for the fact that it is a direct ancestor of today's Book of Moses. Most of its changes were discovered during the preparation of the 1902 edition and were corrected. Only a few continue in today's Pearl of Great Price.

The 1902 Pearl of Great Price

The 1902 edition of the Pearl of Great Price was not a minor updating but a major revision. The most noticeable features are that it deleted material already found in the Doctrine and Covenants (thus it included only what is in the Pearl of Great Price today),[46] and it contained chapters and verses for the first time. It also added headings and cross-referencing foot-

---

46. The poem "Truth" was deleted also.

notes. It was in the 1902 edition that the Pearl of Great Price took on most of the form in which we recognize it now. The 1902 edition also gave us a reworked text of the Book of Moses, a text that has not changed significantly since then.

Joseph Smith's death in 1844 disconnected the Church of Jesus Christ of Latter-day Saints from the New Translation of the Bible. The Prophet was the last Church leader to see the original manuscripts and the only president of the Church ever to be involved in any way with them. No one who worked on the New Translation came west with the Saints,[47] and subsequent Church leaders probably had limited knowledge of it. Over the decades, the absence of information allowed much misunderstanding about the New Translation to make its way into Latter-day Saint culture, a process that would continue into the 1970s. No Latter-day Saint edition of the Book of Moses was prepared with any access to the original JST manuscripts. That placed the Church at a significant disadvantage when it decided to provide a corrected edition in 1902. It is likely that by then, Church leaders had limited knowledge of how our own text of the Book of Moses had been obtained, except in the general understanding that it came from Joseph Smith's Bible translation. It is likely that few, if any, knew then that the Book of Moses came from the RLDS *Inspired Version*, and if so, it is likely that no one knew why. Thus when the 1902 edition was prepared, Church leaders did not have a standard against which they could judge the accuracy of the text.

The preparation of the new Pearl of Great Price, including the revised text of the Book of Moses, was assigned to Professor James E. Talmage of the University of Utah.[48] He used as his beginning text a copy of the 1888 printing, which unfortunately was not carefully done and included both

---

47. Joseph Smith (died 1844), Oliver Cowdery (excommunicated 1838, died in the Church 1850), John Whitmer (excommunicated 1838), Emma Smith (did not go west), Sidney Rigdon (excommunicated 1844), and Frederick G. Williams (excommunicated 1839, died in the Church 1842).

48. See title page, 1902 Pearl of Great Price; Conference Report, October 1902, 83; James E. Talmage Journal, February 2, 1900 (vol. 10, page 327), L. Tom Perry Special Collections, Harold B. Lee Library, Brigham Young University, Provo, Utah.

James E. Talmage Journal, February 2, 1900, detail, recording his assignment from the First Presidency to prepare a new edition of the Pearl of Great Price

typographical errors and other changes. His work on the new edition is docu-
mented in his 1888 copy.[49] On its pages he edited the text, writing corrections to errors in the printing and inserting many new wordings. It was
from his copy that the compositors set the type for the 1902 edition.[50] A
comparison of the available evidence shows the following process at work.
In an effort to produce the best text of the Book of Moses possible, Dr.
Talmage edited his 1888 copy against earlier printings that he apparently
felt were better than what was preserved in the then-current text. Taking in
hand the early texts from *The Evening and the Morning Star* and the *Times
and Seasons,* as well as an 1879 Pearl of Great Price, he edited his text back-
wards to match many of the wordings in those printings. He had no way of
knowing what was on the original manuscripts, and it is likely that he believed that because the newspaper texts were older and were published during the lifetime of Joseph Smith, they contained a more accurate or authori-
tative text than that used by Elder Orson Pratt in 1878. Probably no one
living in Salt Lake City at that time could have known that the 1878 edition was much closer to the words on Joseph Smith's original documents.
In all, Dr. Talmage made about seventy changes that were based on the earlier printings. Following are some examples:

OT1, OT2:	and *as* Moses beheld the world (Moses 1:8)
TS, 1902:	and Moses beheld the world
OT1, OT2:	his glory has been upon me, *and it is glory unto me,* wherefore (Moses 1:18)
TS, 1902:	his glory has been upon me, wherefore
OT1, OT2:	Depart *hence,* Satan (Moses 1:20)
TS, 1902:	Depart *from me,* Satan
OT1, OT2:	he beheld *again* his glory, for it *rested* upon him (Moses 1:25)
TS, 1902:	he beheld his glory *again,* for it *was* upon him

49. James E. Talmage's 1888 Pearl of Great Price is housed in the L. Tom Perry Special
     Collections, Harold B. Lee Library, Brigham Young University.
50. A second, identical copy is also housed in the L. Tom Perry Special Collections. It
     contains Talmage's notations for the cross-reference footnotes of the 1902 edition.

one God only will I worship, which is the God of glory. 2/And now Satan began to tremble, and the earth shook; and Moses received strength, and called upon God, in the name of the Only Begotten, saying to Satan: Depart hence. 22/And it came to pass that Satan cried with a loud voice, with weeping, and wailing, and gnashing of teeth; and departed hence, yea, from the presence of Moses, that he beheld him not.

23 And now of this thing Moses bore record; but because of wickedness it is not had among the children of men. 24/And it came to pass that when Satan had departed from the presence of Moses, that Moses lifted up his eyes unto heaven, being filled with the Holy Ghost, which beareth record of the Father and the Son; 25/and calling upon the name of God, he beheld again his glory, for it rested upon him; and he heard a voice, saying: Blessed art thou, Moses, for I, the Almighty, have chosen thee, and thou shalt be made stronger than many waters; for they shall obey thy command, even as if thou wert God. 26/And lo, I am with thee, even unto the end of thy days; for thou shalt deliver my people from bondage, even Israel my chosen. 27 And it came to pass, as the voice was still speaking, Moses cast his eyes, and beheld the earth, yea, even all of it; and there was not a particle of it which he did not behold, discerning it by the Spirit of God; 28/and he beheld also

the inhabitants thereof, and there was not a soul which he beheld not; and he discerned them by the Spirit of God; and their numbers were great, even as numberless as the sand upon the sea shore. 29/And he beheld many lands; and each land was called earth, and there were inhabitants on the face thereof.

30 And it came to pass that Moses called upon God, saying: Tell me, I pray thee, why these things are so, and by what thou madest them? 31/And behold, the glory of God was upon Moses, so that Moses stood in the presence of God, and talked with him face to face; and the Lord God said unto Moses: For mine own purpose have I made these things. Here is wisdom, and it remaineth in me. 32/And by the word of my power have I created them, which is mine Only Begotten Son, who is full of grace and truth. 33/And worlds without number have I created; and I also created them for mine own purpose; and by the Son I created them, which is mine Only Begotten. 34/And the first man of all men have I called Adam, which is many. 35/But only an account of this earth, and the inhabitants thereof, give I unto you. For behold, there are many worlds that have passed away by the word of my power. And there are many now stand, and innumerable are they unto man; but all things are numbered unto me, for they are mine, and I know them.

James E. Talmage's 1888 Pearl of Great Price, pages 4–5, showing his editing in preparation for the 1902 edition, including inserted verse numbers and letters for cross-reference footnotes; Moses 1:20–35

OT1, OT2:	among *even* as many as shall believe (Moses 1:41)
TS, 1902:	among as many as shall believe

OT1, OT2:	Go *forth* to this people (Moses 7:10)
EMS, 1902:	Go to this people

OT1:	land out of the *depths* of the sea (Moses 7:14)
EMS, 1902:	land out of the *depth* of the sea

OT2:	and thou art there (Moses 7:30)
EMS, 1902:	and *yet* thou art there

OT2:	*has* pled before my face (Moses 7:39)
EMS, 1902:	*hath* plead before my face

OT1:	he saw great *tribulation* (Moses 7:66)
EMS, 1902:	he saw great *tribulations*

In addition to the changes made to match earlier publications of Book of Moses material, Professor Talmage made over thirty revisions that are not based on any previous printing or any known manuscript. A few of those changes correct the grammar or bring the wording more in line with contemporary style:

OT1, OT2, 1878:	Behold I, send me (Moses 4:1)
1902:	Behold, *here am* I, send me

OT1, OT2:	see thou *show* them unto no man (Moses 4:32)
1878:	see thou *showest* them unto no man
1902:	see thou *show* them unto no man

OT1, OT2, 1878:	the Lord cursed . . . all *they* that had covenanted with Satan (Moses 5:52)
1902:	the Lord cursed . . . all *them* that had covenanted with Satan

OT1, OT2, 1878:	and *an* Hell have I prepared (Moses 6:29)
1902:	and *a* Hell have I prepared

Most changes show editorial preferences that differ from the wording Joseph Smith dictated to his scribes:

them; and Enoch continued his preaching in righteousness unto the people of God. And it came to pass in his days, that he built a city that was called the City of Holiness: even Zion. And it came to pass that Enoch talked with the Lord; and he said unto the Lord, Surely Zion shall dwell in safety forever. But the Lord said unto Enoch, Zion have I blessed, but the residue of the people have I cursed. And it came to pass that the Lord showed unto Enoch all the inhabitants of the earth; and he beheld, and lo, Zion, in process of time, was taken up into heaven. And the Lord said unto Enoch, Behold mine abode forever.

And Enoch also beheld the residue of the people which were the sons of Adam; and they were a mixture of all the seed of Adam, save it were the seed of Cain, for the seed of Cain were black, and had not place among them. And after that Zion was taken up into heaven, Enoch beheld, and, lo, all the nations of the earth were before him; and there came generation upon generation; and Enoch was high and lifted up, even in the bosom of the Father, and the Son of Man; and behold, the power of Satan was upon all the face of the earth. And he saw angels descending out of heaven; and he heard a loud voice, saying, Wo, wo be unto the inhabitants of the earth. And he beheld Satan; and he had a great chain in his hand, and it veiled the whole

face of the earth with darkness; and he looked up and laughed, and his angels rejoiced. And Enoch beheld angels descending out of heaven, bearing testimony of the Father and the Son; and the Holy Ghost fell on many, and they were caught up by the power of heaven into Zion. And it came to pass that the God of heaven looked upon the residue of the people, and wept; and Enoch bore record of it, saying, How is it that the heavens weep, and shed forth their tears as the rain upon the mountains? And Enoch said unto the Lord, How is it that thou canst weep, seeing thou art holy, and from all eternity to all eternity? And were it possible that man could number the particles of the earth, yea millions of earths like this, it would not be a beginning to the number of thy creations; and thy curtains are stretched out still; and thou art there, and thy bosom is there; and also thou art just; thou art merciful and kind forever; thou hast taken Zion to thine own bosom, from all thy creations, from all eternity to all eternity; and naught but peace, justice, and truth is the habitation of thy throne; and mercy shall go before thy face and have no end; how is it that thou canst weep?

The Lord said unto Enoch, Behold these thy brethren; they are the workmanship of mine own hands; and I gave unto them their knowledge, in the day that I created them; and in the garden

James E. Talmage's 1888 Pearl of Great Price, pages 38–39, showing his editing in preparation for the 1902 edition, including inserted verse numbers and letters for cross-reference footnotes; Moses 7:18–32

OT2, 1878:   and beheld the earth, yea, even all *the face* of it (Moses 1:27)

1902:   and beheld the earth, yea, even all of it

OT1, OT2, 1878: the glory of *God* was upon Moses (Moses 1:31)

1902:   the glory of *the Lord* was upon Moses

OT1, OT2, 1878: Adam called upon the name of the Lord, *and Eve also, his wife* (Moses 5:4)

1902:   Adam *and Eve, his wife,* called upon the name of the Lord

OT1, 1878:   yea *and* millions of earths (Moses 7:30)

1902:   yea millions of earths

OT1, OT2, 1878: How is it *that* thou canst weep? (Moses 7:31)

1902:   How is it thou canst weep?

OT1, OT2, 1878: and Enoch saw Noah, *also*, and his family (Moses 7:42)

1902:   and Enoch *also* saw Noah, and his family

OT1, OT2, 1878: And as Enoch saw *thus*, he had bitterness of soul (Moses 7:44)

1902:   And as Enoch saw *this*, he had bitterness of soul

OT1, 1878:   For *inasmuch* as (Moses 7:59)

1902:   *Forasmuch* as

OT1, OT2, 1878: for the space of a thousand years *shall* the earth rest (Moses 7:64)

1902:   for the space of a thousand years the earth *shall* rest

OT1, OT2, 1878: the sons of men saw that *their* daughters were fair (Moses 8:14)

1902:   the sons of men saw that *those* daughters were fair

OT1, OT2, 1878: even as our fathers *did*, and ye shall (Moses 8:24)

1902:   even as our fathers, and ye shall

A few changes in the 1902 edition were not written by Dr. Talmage in his copy of the Pearl of Great Price and are not based on any earlier manuscript

saying: Of every tree of the garden thou mayest freely eat,ᵍ

17. But of the tree of the knowledge of good and evil,ʰ thou shalt not eat of it;ⁱ nevertheless, thou mayest choose for thyself,ʲ for it is given unto thee; but, remember that I forbid it, for in the day thou eatest thereof thou shalt surely die.ᵏ

18. And I, the Lord God, said unto mine Only Begotten,ˡ that it was not good that the man should be alone; wherefore, I will make an helpmeet for him.ᵐ

19.ⁿ And out of the ground I, the Lord God, formed every beast of the field, and every fowl of the air; and commanded that they should come unto Adam, to see what he would call them; and they were also living souls;ᵒ for I, God, breathed into them the breath of life, and commanded that whatsoever Adam called every living creature, that should be the name thereof.

20. And Adam gave names to all cattle, and to the fowl of the air, and to every beast of the field; but as for Adam, there was not found an helpmeet for him.

21.ᵖ And I, the Lord God, caused a deep sleep to fall upon Adam; and he slept, and I took one of his ribs and closed up the flesh in the stead thereof;

22. And the rib which I, the Lord God, had taken from man, made I a woman, and brought her unto the man.

23. And Adam said: This I know now is bone of my bones, and flesh of my flesh; she shall be called Woman, because she was taken out of man.

g, verse 9. h, 4:10. i, compare 4:3; 6:53, 56; 7:32; compare Doc. and Cov. 29:35; II Nephi 2:27; 10:23; Alma 12:31; 30:48; Helaman 14:31. j, 4:3; Abraham 5:13. k, verse 29; Abraham 5:14. l, compare verses 19 and 20 with Abraham 5:9, 21, and with Genesis 2:18. m, compare Abraham 5:14. n, see verse 7. o, compare verses 21-25 inclusive with Abraham 5:15-19; and with Genesis 2:21-25.

24. Therefore shall a man leave his father and his mother, and shall cleave unto his wife; and they shall be one flesh.

25. And they were both naked, the man and his wife, and were not ashamed.ᶻ

CHAPTER IV.

1. And I, the Lord God, spakeᵃ unto Moses, saying: That Satan,ᵇ whom thou hast commanded in the name of mine Only Begotten,ᶜ is the same which was from the beginning,ᵈ and he came before me, saying—Behold, here am I, send me, I will be thy son, and I will redeem all mankind, that one soul shall not be lost, and surely I will do it; wherefore give me thine honor.ᵉ

2. But, behold, my Beloved Son,ᶠ which was my Beloved and Chosenᵍ from the beginning,ʰ said unto me—Father, thy will be done, and the glory be thine forever.ⁱ

3. Wherefore, because that Satan rebelled against me,ʲ and sought to destroy the agency of man,ᵏ which I, the Lord God, had given him, and also, that I should give unto him mine own power; by the power of mine Only Begotten,ˡ I caused that he should be cast down;ᵐ

4. And he became Satan,ⁿ yea, even the devil, the father of all lies,ᵒ to deceive and to blind men,

z, 4:13, 16, 17, 27.

a, 1:1. b, 1:12. c, 1:17; see also 1:6; compare Doc. and Cov. 29:38; 76:25, 28. d, compare Abraham 3:24; Writings of Joseph Smith, 2:17; compare Matthew 3:17; Mark 1:11; Luke 9:35; III Nephi 11:7. e, 4:1; 25:7; 2a. f, 4:2; see 6:57. g, compare Abraham 3:27. h, Abraham 3:28. i, 1:32; see also 1:6. j, Doc. and Cov. 29:36; 76:25-27. k, compare 6:24; II Nephi 2:18; Doc. and Cov. 10:25; 93:29, 35. l, 1:12.

1902 Pearl of Great Price, pages 14–15; Moses 3:16–4:4

or printing. These may have resulted from insertions he or others made in the printer's proofs, but more likely they are errors made by a typesetter.

OT2, 1878:	where I, the Lord, created much gold (Moses 3:11)
1902:	where I, the Lord *God*, created much gold
OT1, 1878:	sent forth in the world, unto the *end* thereof (Moses 6:30)
1902:	sent forth in the world, unto the *ends* thereof
OT2, 1878:	the filthiness which *has* gone forth out of me (Moses 7:48)
1902:	the filthiness which *is* gone forth out of me

The punctuation of the 1902 Book of Moses generally follows that of the 1888 printing. But there are some differences, many of which were caused by the insertion of verse breaks. The 1921 and 1981 editions follow the 1902 punctuation virtually without change.[51]

---

51. We do not know what Dr. Talmage's instructions were for the 1902 Book of Moses. His journal mentions his work on the new edition and related meetings on several occasions, but with little detail. Almost all of the changes made in the 1902 edition remain in the Book of Moses today. In the October 1902 general conference, President Joseph F. Smith presented the newly published edition of the Pearl of Great Price for a sustaining vote, and it was reaffirmed in its place as one of the standard works of the Church. President Smith stated: "I hold in my hand a copy of the revised edition of the Pearl of Great Price. The Pearl of Great Price, as it originally existed, was presented before the general conference and accepted as one of the standard works of the Church. Since then the book has undergone a revision; that is to say, all the revelations that it formerly contained which were also in the Book of Doctrine and Covenants, have been eliminated from it. . . . In addition to this, Professor James E. Talmage has gone through the work and divided it into chapters and verses, making it a far more convenient book of reference than it was before. He has also supplied copious footnotes or references, which will be an aid in the study of the book. These are the changes that have been made in the book, and we now present this book in its revised form—the original matter being preserved as it was before, only divided into chapters and verses—for your acceptance as a standard work

The 1921 and 1981 Pearl of Great Price

The 1921 edition of the Pearl of Great Price was prepared under the direction of a committee of members of the Quorum of the Twelve Apostles, including Elder James E. Talmage.[52] The most visible change in that edition was the two-column format, which had been the norm in Bible printings for centuries and was now adopted in the Pearl of Great Price. The text of the Book of Moses underwent only small changes. Most of the changes were orthographic or typographical and had little bearing on the choice or meaning of words, as these examples show:

1902:	I will make an *helpmeet* for him (Moses 3:18, 20)
1921:	I will make an *help meet* for him
1902:	and they sewed *fig leaves* together (Moses 4:13)
1921:	and they sewed *fig-leaves* together
1902:	henceforth and *for ever* (Moses 5:9; 6:66)
1921:	henceforth and *forever*

One change corrects an error from the 1902 edition:

1902:	*and* they were despised among all people (Moses 7:8)
1921:	*that* they were despised among all people

The 1981 Pearl of Great Price is the one used in the Church today. It was part of an extensive project that produced new editions of all the scriptures, including a new Latter-day Saint Bible edition published in 1979. New editions of the Book of Mormon, the Doctrine and Covenants, and the Pearl of Great Price were published together in 1981.[53] In addition to new footnotes and headings, the new Pearl of Great Price included small changes to the text. In the Book of Moses, only four changes were made in

---

of the Church" (Conference Report, October 1902, 83; see also James E. Talmage Journal, October 6, 1902 [vol. 10, page 471], L. Tom Perry Special Collections).

52. Elder Talmage was called to the Quorum of the Twelve Apostles in December 1911.

53. See Robert J. Matthews, "The New Publications of the Standard Works—1979, 1981," *BYU Studies* 22, no. 4 (Fall 1982): 387–423.

were crowned at the right hand of the Son of Man,⁵⁷ with crowns of glory;

57. And as many of the spirits as were in prison⁵⁸ came forth, and stood on the right hand of God; and the remainder were reserved in chains of darkness until the judgment of the great day.

58. And again Enoch wept and cried unto the Lord, saying: When shall the earth rest?⁵⁹

59. And Enoch beheld the Son of Man ascend up unto the Father; and he called unto the Lord, saying: Wilt thou not come again upon the earth? Forasmuch as thou art God, and I know thee, and thou hast sworn unto me,⁶⁰ and commanded me that I should ask in the name of thine Only Begotten; thou hast made me, and given unto me a right to thy throne, and not of myself, but through thine own grace; wherefore, I ask thee if thou wilt not come again on the earth.

60. And the Lord said⁶¹ unto Enoch: As I live, even so will I come in the last days, in the days of wickedness and vengeance, to fulfil the oath which I have made unto you⁶² concerning the children of Noah;

61. And the day shall come that the earth shall rest, but before that day the heavens shall be darkened, and a veil of darkness shall cover the earth; and the heavens shall shake, and also the earth; and great tribulations shall be among the children of men, but my people will I preserve;

62. And righteousness will I send down out of heaven; and truth will I send forth out of the earth,⁶³ to bear testimony of mine Only Begotten;⁶⁴ his resurrection from the dead; yea, and also the resurrection of all men; and righteousness and truth will I cause to sweep the earth as with a flood, to gather out mine elect from the four quarters of the earth, unto a place which I shall prepare, an Holy City, that my people may gird up their loins, and be looking forth for the time of my coming; for there shall be my tabernacle, and it shall be called Zion,⁶⁵ a New Jerusalem.⁶⁶

63. And the Lord said unto Enoch: Then shalt thou and all thy city⁶⁷ meet them there, and we will receive them into our bosom, and they shall see us; and we will fall upon their necks, and they shall fall upon our necks, and we will kiss each other;

64. And there shall be mine abode,⁶⁸ and it shall be Zion, which shall come forth out of all the creations which I have made; and for the space of a thousand years⁶⁹ the earth shall rest.

65. And it came to pass that Enoch saw the day of the coming of the Son of Man,⁷⁰ in the last days, to dwell on the earth in righteousness for the space of a thousand years;⁷¹

66. But before that day he saw great tribulations among the wicked; and he also saw the sea, that it was troubled, and men's hearts failing them, looking forth with fear for the judgments of the Almighty God, which should come upon the wicked.

67. And the Lord showed

p. 56a, ver. 24. 49:9. 61:4. 1 Pet. 3:18—20.
44, 1:1. 48a, ver. 44. 59a, compare ver. 16.
Ith. 11:5—3. ... 62a, compare ver. 6. Rev. 3:12, 21:2, 10.
40-42, 12:1, 4. 6a, compare ver. 21. 4a, ver. 51.
5e, ver. 64.

Enoch all things, even unto the end of the world; and he saw the day of the righteous, the hour of their redemption; and received a fulness of joy;⁷²

68. And all the days of Zion,⁷³ in the days of Enoch, were three hundred and sixty-five years.

69. And Enoch and all his people walked with God, and he dwelt in the midst of Zion; and it came to pass that Zion was not, for God received it up into his own bosom; and from thence went forth the saying, Zion is Fled.⁷⁴

CHAPTER 8.

THE WRITINGS OF MOSES

As received by Joseph Smith the Prophet, in December 1830. Concluded.

1. And all the days of Enoch were four hundred and thirty years.

2. And it came to pass that Methuselah, the son of Enoch, was not taken, that the covenants of the Lord might be fulfilled, which he made to Enoch;¹ for he truly covenanted with Enoch that Noah should be of the fruit of his loins.

3. And it came to pass that Methuselah prophesied that from his loins should spring all the kingdoms of the earth (through Noah), and he took glory unto himself.

4. And there came forth a great famine into the land, and the Lord cursed the earth with a sore curse, and many of the inhabitants thereof died.

5.² And it came to pass that Methuselah lived one hundred and eighty-seven years, and begat Lamech;

6. And Methuselah lived, after he begat Lamech, seven hundred and eighty-two years, and begat sons and daughters;

7. And all the days of Methuselah were nine hundred and sixty-nine years, and he died.

8. And Lamech lived one hundred and eighty-two years, and begat a son,

9. And he called his name Noah,³ saying: This son shall comfort us concerning our work and toil of our hands, because of the ground which the Lord hath cursed.⁴

10. And Lamech lived, after he begat Noah, five hundred and ninety-five years, and begat sons and daughters;

11. And all the days of Lamech were seven hundred and seventy-seven years, and he died.

12. And Noah was four hundred and fifty years old, and begat Japheth; and forty-two years afterward he begat Shem of her who was the mother of Japheth, and when he was five hundred years old he begat Ham.⁵

13. And Noah and his sons hearkened⁶ unto the Lord, and gave heed, and they were called the sons of God.

14. And when these men began to multiply on the face of the earth, and daughters were born unto them, the sons of men⁷ saw that those daughters were fair, and they took them wives, even as they chose.

15. And the Lord said⁸ unto Noah: The daughters of thy sons have sold themselves; for behold mine anger is kindled⁹ against the sons of men,¹⁰ for they will not hearken to my voice.

16. And it came to pass that

Chap. 8, ver. 2:35. 5a, 6:34. 3b, ver. 2:1. Compare Gen. 5:24.
1:1. 4a, ver. 2:36. e, compare 5:19. d, compare vers. 5—12 with Gen. 5:25—31. 3b, verse by verse. c, 7:42. e, Abraham 1:24.
Gen. 5:29. b, 6:38, verse by verse. 9a, compare Gen. 6:1, 2. b, 5:22. 1, 4:3.
mn, 6:27.   h, 5:32,   o, 4:4.   Compare 6:14.

the wording. An error was corrected that had entered the Pearl of Great Price in 1902, having been copied from the 1843 *Times and Seasons* printing:

OT1, OT2:   *transfigured* before him (Moses 1:14)

TS, 1902, 1921:   *strengthened* before him

1981:   *transfigured* before him

The 1981 edition dealt with an enigmatic word in Moses 1:19. Oliver Cowdery wrote Joseph Smith's dictation as follows: "Satan cried with a loud voice and *wrent* upon the earth." The words were copied identically on OT2 by John Whitmer, but Whitmer wrote "rent" on another copy that he made of the manuscript.[54] *Wrent* is likely a regional spelling of *rent,* the past tense of *rend,* "to tear." Satan "tore upon the earth." In the Printer's Manuscript of the Book of Mormon, copied by Oliver Cowdery from the Original Manuscript, the word *wrent* is found at Alma 14:27, "the walls of the prison were *wrent* in twain," and at 3 Nephi 8:18, "the rocks were *wrent* in twain."[55] In the 1830 Book of Mormon, the spelling of the first of these remained "wrent," but the spelling of the second was standardized to "rent." *Wrent* also appears elsewhere in the Joseph Smith Translation, as a noun at Mark 2:21, "the *wrent* is made worse."[56] John Whitmer was the scribe for that section.[57] In the RLDS Committee Manuscript at Moses 1:19, Joseph Smith III's hand-writing is not clear, but it appears that he wrote "went" rather than "wrent," probably following the reading in the *Times and Seasons.* The typesetter clearly saw "went" and rendered the word thus in the 1867 *Inspired Version.* Elder Orson Pratt changed it back to "rent" in the 1878 Pearl of Great Price, and so it remained until the 1981 edition, when it was changed to "ranted."[58]

---

54. Old Testament Manuscript 3, page 1, line 44.

55. Royal Skousen, ed., *The Printer's Manuscript of the Book of Mormon: Typographical Facsimile of the Entire Text in Two Parts* (Provo, UT: Foundation for Ancient Research and Mormon Studies, Brigham Young University, 2001), 462, 804. The Original Manuscript pages containing these passage are no longer extant.

56. New Testament Manuscript 2, Folio 2, page 12, line 2.

57. I thank Robert J. Matthews for bringing these uses of the word *wrent* to my attention.

58. Noah Webster's 1828 dictionary cites a source that uses *rent* (present tense) as a verb with the meaning "rant"; *An American Dictionary of the English Language* (New York: S. Converse, 1828), s.v. "rent."

the garden, in the cool of the day; and Adam and his wife went to hide themselves from the "presence of the Lord God amongst the trees of the garden.

15 And I, the Lord God, called unto Adam, and said unto him: Where "goest thou?

16 And he said: I heard thy voice in the garden, and I was afraid, because I beheld that I was naked, and I hid myself.

17 And I, the Lord God, said unto Adam: Who told thee thou wast naked? Hast thou eaten of the tree whereof I commanded thee that thou shouldst not eat, if so thou shouldst surely "die?

18 And the man said: The woman thou gavest me, and commandest that she should remain with me, she gave me of the fruit of the tree and I did eat.

19 And I, the Lord God, said unto the woman: What is this thing which thou hast done? And the woman said: The serpent "beguiled me, and I did eat.

20 And I, the Lord God, said unto the serpent: Because thou hast done this thou shalt be "cursed above all cattle, and above every beast of the field; upon thy belly shalt thou go, and dust shalt thou eat all the days of thy life;

21 And I will put "enmity between thee and the woman, between thy seed and her seed; and he shall "bruise thy head, and thou shalt bruise his heel.

22 Unto the woman, I, the Lord God, said: I will greatly multiply thy sorrow and thy conception. In "sorrow thou shalt bring forth children, and thy desire shall be to thy "husband, and he shall rule over thee.

23 And unto Adam, I, the Lord God, said: Because thou hast hearkened unto the voice of thy wife, and hast eaten of the fruit of the tree of which I commanded thee, saying—Thou shalt not eat of it, "cursed shall be the ground for thy sake; in "sorrow shalt thou eat of it all the days of thy life.

24 Thorns also, and thistles shall it bring forth to thee, and thou shalt eat the herb of the field.

25 By the "sweat of thy "face shalt thou eat bread, until thou shalt return unto the ground—for thou out of it wast taken: for "dust thou wast, and unto dust shalt thou return.

26 And Adam called his wife's name Eve, because she was the mother of all living; for thus have I, the Lord God, called the first of all women, which are "many.

27 Unto Adam, and also unto his wife, did I, the Lord God, make coats of "skins, and "clothed them.

28 And I, the Lord God, "said unto mine Only Begotten: Behold, the "man is become as one of us to "know good and evil; and now lest he put forth his hand and "partake also of the "tree of life, and eat and live forever,

29 Therefore I, the Lord God, will send him forth from the Garden of "Eden, to till the ground from whence he was taken;

30 For as I, the Lord God, liveth, even so my "words cannot return

14b Jonah 1:3.
15a Gen. 3:9.
17a Moses 3:17.
19a Gen. 3:13 (1-13).
  2 Ne. 9:9; Mosiah 16:3; Ether 8:25.
20a Gen. 3:14 (13-16).
21a Gen. 3:15.
  b Ps. 68:21; Rom. 16:20; Moses 3:7; 6:59; Abr. 5:7.
22a Gen. 3:16; 4:7.
  b TC Marriage, Husbands; Marriage, Wives.
23a Job 14:1; Moses 8:9. TC Earth, Curse of.
  b TC Suffering.
25a Gen. 3:19 (17-19). TC Mortality.
  b Moses 5:1.
  c Gen. 2:7; Job 10:9; Ps. 104:29; Alma 42:30; Moses 3:7; 6:59; Abr. 5:7.
26a Gen. 3:20.
27a Gen. 27:16; Alma 49:6.
  b TC Apparel; Clothing; Modesty.
28a Gen. 3:22.
  b TC Man, Potential to Become Like Heavenly Father.
  c TC Knowledge; Probation.
  d Alma 42:5 (4-5).
  e Gen. 2:9; 1 Ne. 11:25; Moses 3:9; Abr. 5:9.
29a TC Eden.
30a 1 Kgs. 8:56; Jer. 44:28.

void, for as they go forth out of my mouth they must be fulfilled.

31 So I drove out the man, and I placed at the east of the Garden of "Eden, "Cherubim, and a flaming sword, which turned every way, to keep the way of the tree of life.

32 (And these are the words which I spake unto my servant Moses, and they are true even as I will; and I have spoken them unto you. See thou show them unto no man, until I command you, except to them that believe. Amen.)

CHAPTER 5
(June-October 1830)

Adam and Eve bring forth children—Adam offers sacrifice, serves God—Cain and "Abel born—Cain rebels, loves Satan more than God, and becomes Perdition—Murder and wickedness spread—The gospel preached from the beginning.

AND it came to pass that after I, the Lord God, had driven them out, that Adam began to till the earth, and to have "dominion over all the beasts of the field, and to eat his bread by the sweat of his "brow, as the Lord had commanded him. And Eve, also, his wife, did "labor with him.

2 And "Adam knew his wife, and she bare unto him "sons and "daughters, and they began to "multiply and to replenish the earth.

3 And from that time forth, the sons and "daughters of Adam began to divide two and two in the land, and to till the land, and to tend flocks, and they also begat sons and daughters.

4 And Adam and Eve, his wife, called upon the name of the Lord, and they heard the voice of the Lord from the way toward the Garden of "Eden, speaking unto them, and they saw him not; for they were shut out from his "presence.

5 And he gave unto them commandments, that they should "worship the Lord their God, and should offer the "firstlings of their flocks, for an offering unto the Lord. And Adam was "obedient unto the commandments of the Lord.

6 And after many days an "angel of the Lord appeared unto Adam, saying: Why dost thou offer "sacrifices unto the Lord? And Adam said unto him: I know not, save the Lord commanded me.

7 And then the angel spake, saying: This thing is a "similitude of the "sacrifice of the Only Begotten of the Father, which is full of "grace and "truth.

8 Wherefore, thou shalt do all that thou doest in the "name of the Son, and thou shalt "repent and "call upon God in the name of the Son forevermore.

9 And in that day the "Holy Ghost fell upon Adam, which beareth record of the Father and the Son, saying: I am the "Only Begotten of the Father from the beginning, henceforth and forever, that as thou hast "fallen thou mayest be "re-

31a TC Eden.
  b TC Cherubim.
5 1a Moses 2:26.
  b Moses 4:25.
2a Gen. 5:4 (3-32).
  b Gen. 4:1 (1-2); Moses 5:16 (16-17).
  c D&C 138:39.
  d Gen. 9:1; Moses 2:28.
3a Gen. 4:17; Moses 5:28.
4a Gen. 4:26; Moses 6:4.
  b TC Eden.
  c Alma 42:9.
5a TC Worship.
b Ex. 13:12 (12-13); Num. 18:17; Mosiah 2:3. TC Firstborn.
  c Moses 5:19 (19-20).
6a TC Angels.
  b TC Obedience; Sacrifice.
7a TC Jesus Christ, Types, in Anticipation.
  b Gen. 4:5 (3-7); 1 Chr. 6:49; Alma 34:10 (10-15); Moses 5:21 (20-26). TC Blood, Symbolism of; Jesus Christ, Atonement through.
c Moses 1:32. TC Grace.
  d Moses 1:6.
8a Moses 1:17.
  b Moses 6:57; 7:10.
  c TC Repentance.
  d TC Prayer.
9a TC Holy Ghost, Baptism of.
  b TC Jesus Christ, Divine Sonship.
  c TC Death, Spiritual, First; Fall of Man.
  d Ps. 49:15; Mosiah 27:24 (24-29); D&C 93:38. TC Christ; TC Redemption; Salvation, Plan of.

OT1, OT2:	Satan cried with a loud voice and *wrent* upon the earth (Moses 1:19)
TS, CM, *IV*:	Satan cried with a loud voice and *went* upon the earth
1878, 1902, 1921:	Satan cried with a loud voice and *rent* upon the earth
1981:	Satan cried with a loud voice and *ranted* upon the earth

At Moses 4:18, the 1981 edition of the Pearl of Great Price changes the tense of one word:

OT1:	thou . . . *commanded* that she should (Moses 4:18)
1878, 1902, 1921:	thou . . . *commandedst* that she should
1981:	thou . . . *commandest* that she should

The deletion of the second letter *d* avoids a difficult consonant cluster, yet it changes the tense of the clause from the past to the present.

The final word change in the 1981 Book of Moses revises the phrase "save it were" to "save it was" (Moses 7:22). The phrase "save it were"—meaning "except for"—appears seventy-six times in the Book of Mormon, once in the Doctrine and Covenants (see D&C 18:35), and once elsewhere ten verses earlier in the Book of Moses (see Moses 7:12).[59]

OT1, OT2:	save it *were* (Moses 7:22)
1878, 1902, 1921:	save it *were*
1981:	save it *was*

The 1981 edition also moves the verse break between Moses 5:52 and 5:53. The sentence "And it was among the sons of men" began verse 53 in the 1902 and 1921 editions. In the 1981 edition, it was placed at the end of verse 52.

---

59. The related phrase "save it be" appears in the Book of Mormon forty-seven times (for example, 2 Nephi 2:8) and nine times in the Doctrine and Covenants (for example, D&C 18:20).

HISTORICAL TEXT

The following is a transcription of the Book of Moses, Genesis 1:1–6:13, from Old Testament Manuscript 2 (OT2), Joseph Smith's final draft of his New Translation of Genesis. It is found on pages 1–27 of that manuscript. The Prophet first dictated this part of Genesis between June 1830 and February 1831. Oliver Cowdery, John Whitmer, Emma Smith, and Sidney Rigdon assisted him as scribes. In the original dictated manuscript, Old Testament Manuscript 1 (OT1), the Book of Moses material is found on pages 1–21. The present manuscript (OT2) is a copy of the original, made by John Whitmer in March 1831. With very few exceptions, OT2 was the document on which Joseph Smith continued to refine the translation. He added to it numerous insertions and corrections, dictating them primarily to his scribe Sidney Rigdon. The present transcription preserves carefully the words of the manuscript, including words inserted after the original writing. Unless otherwise noted, the handwriting is that of John Whitmer.

The footnotes in the Historical Text show the history of the words from the original manuscripts to the current (1981) edition of the Pearl of Great Price. They include all the manuscripts and editions of the Book of Moses that comprise the genealogy of today's text, and they also include the early printings in Latter-day Saint periodicals and elsewhere from which later editions sometimes drew textual changes.

Editorial Procedures[1]

- Punctuation marks, which were added by unidentified hands after the text was written, are represented without change. Where revisions were made in punctuation, only the final punctuation is shown.
- Canceled text, whether written over or removed through erasure or strikeout, is shown lined out (for example, ~~word~~).
- Scribal insertions are shown in angle brackets (for example, <word>).
- Letters from canceled words that were reused as part of inserted words are shown as deleted and inserted (for example, ~~was~~ <were> instead of wa~~s~~<ere>).
- Errors corrected by scribes in their own writing are not shown. Insertions made by scribes to correct their own writing are not identified as insertions.
- Original line endings have been retained. When a line of text is too long for the available space, subsequent text is indented.
- Original capitalization has been retained. Where revisions were made in capitalization, only the final capitalization is shown.
- Spelling has been standardized to modern usage; spelling of names has been made consistent with spelling in the King James translation; numerals have been spelled out in standard style.
- Ampersands (&) have been replaced with "and."
- Hyphenation has been standardized to modern usage. In the footnotes, hyphenation differences in numbers are ignored (for example, "sixty-five" or "sixty five").
- Footnotes make reference to the entire immediately preceding correction (deletion and insertion) or to the immediately preceding word, unless otherwise indicated.
- Footnotes not attached to existing words in the text are shown with a backslash (for example, \[1]).

---

1. More complex transcriptions that reflect the original spelling and the full history of scribal activity are found in Scott H. Faulring, Kent P. Jackson, and Robert J. Matthews, eds., *Joseph Smith's New Translation of the Bible: Original Manuscripts* (Provo, UT: Religious Studies Center, Brigham Young University, 2004).

- Chapter and verse numbers inserted by nineteenth-century clerks are not represented, nor are marks in the text that show verse breaks. Modern chapter and verse numbers in the Book of Moses (introduced in the 1902 edition) have been inserted in brackets.

Abbreviations

Scribal hands are identified in bold:

ES	Emma Smith
FGW	Frederick G. Williams
JS	Joseph Smith
JW	John Whitmer
OC	Oliver Cowdery
SR	Sidney Rigdon

Manuscripts and editions from which today's Book of Moses derives (in chronological order):

OT1	Old Testament Manuscript 1, dictated by Joseph Smith to **OC**, **JW**, **ES**, and **SR**, June 1830 to February 1831
OT2	Old Testament Manuscript 2, transcribed by **JW** from OT1 March 1831; revised by Joseph Smith with **SR** as scribe; some small corrections recorded by **JS**, **FGW**, and unidentified hands
CM	Final edit of the Committee Manuscript, transcribed by the Reorganized Church of Jesus Christ of Latter Day Saints publication committee from OT1 and OT2 in preparation for the printing of the 1867 *Inspired Version*
IV	1867 *Inspired Version*, published by the Reorganized Church of Jesus Christ of Latter Day Saints, Independence, Missouri, typeset from CM
1878	1878 edition of the Book of Moses, Pearl of Great Price, copied with very little change from *IV*, Salt Lake City, Utah

1888	1888 printing of the 1878 edition of the Book of Moses, Salt Lake City, Utah
1902	1902 edition of the Book of Moses, Salt Lake City, Utah
1921	1921 edition of the Book of Moses, Salt Lake City, Utah
1981	1981 edition of the Book of Moses, Salt Lake City, Utah

Early printings of the Book of Moses that are not part of the direct lineage of today's text but that were consulted by later editors:

(*EMS*)	*The Evening and the Morning Star*, Independence, Missouri
	Vol. 1, no. 3 (August 1832): 2–3 (Moses 7)
	Vol. 1, no. 10 (March 1833): 1 (Moses 6:43–68)
	Vol. 1, no. 11 (April 1833): 1–2 (Moses 5:1–16; 8:13–30)
(LF)	"Lectures on Faith," 1835, Kirtland, Ohio
(*TS*)	*Times and Seasons*, Nauvoo, Illinois
	Vol. 4, no. 5 (January 16, 1843): 71–73 (Moses 1)
(1851)	1851 *Pearl of Great Price*, Liverpool, England
(1879)	1879 printing of the 1878 edition of the Book of Moses, Liverpool, England

The footnotes show the development of readings from one source to the next, in chronological order. Because the early printings are not part of that lineal succession, the citations are shown in parentheses.

MOSES 1

OT2 Page 1 (Moses 1:1–15)

\\[1] [1] The words of God which he spake unto Moses, at a[2] time when
Moses was caught up into an exceeding[3] high mountain, [2] and he saw
God face to face, and he talked with him, and the glory of God was upon
~~Moses~~ <him>[4]; therefore ~~Moses~~ <he>[5] could endure his presence[6], [3] and
    God spake unto Moses,
saying, Behold I[7] am the Lord God Almighty, and endless is my name
for I am without beginning of days or end of years; and is this not[8] endless.
[4] and Behold thou art my Son, Wherefore, look, and I will show[9] thee[10] the
workmanship of mine hands, but not all; for my works are with-
out end, and also my words, for they never cease; [5] wherefore, no man can

---

1. JW handwriting begins
2. (1851) "the"
3. 1921 "exceedingly", followed by 1981
4. **SR** : not in (*TS*), (1851), CM, *IV*, 1878, 1888, 1902, 1921, 1981
5. **SR** : not in (*TS*), (1851), CM, *IV*, 1878, 1888, 1902, 1921, 1981
6. "The words of God . . . endure his presence" title in (1851)
7. "Behold I" : OT1 "Behold I I"
8. "is this not" : (*TS*), (1851), CM "is not this", followed by *IV*, 1878, 1888, 1902, 1921, 1981
9. Archaic spelling "shew" on manuscript modernized throughout to "show" in (*TS*), CM, followed by *IV*, 1878, 1888, 1902, 1921, 1981
10. (Not in *TS*)

Old Testament Manuscript 2, page 1, detail; handwriting of John Whitmer, corrections by Sidney Rigdon; Moses 1:9–15

Behold all my work[11] except he behold all my Glory; and no man can
behold all my glory, and afterwards remain in the flesh <on the earth>[12].
    [6] and I have a
work for thee, Moses, my Son; and thou art in the[13] similitude ~~to~~ <of>[14]
    mine
only begotten; and mine[15] only begotten is and shall be <the Savior>[16], for
    he is full of
grace and truth; but there is none other[17] God beside[18] me; and all
things are present with me, for I know them all. [7] and[19] now Behold
this one thing I show unto thee, Moses, my Son; for thou art
in the World, and now I show it \[20] thee. [8] And it came to pass, that
Moses looked, and beheld the world upon which he was Created, and as[21]
Moses beheld the World and the ends thereof and all the Children of
men which ~~was~~ <are>[22] and which ~~was~~ <were>[23] created, of the same he
    greatly marveled
and wondered, [9] and the presence of God withdrew from Moses, that
    his glory
was not upon ~~Moses~~ <him>[24] and Moses was left unto himself and as he was
left unto himself he fell unto the Earth. [10] And it came to pass

---

11. OT1 "works", followed by (*TS*), (1851), CM, *IV*, 1878, 1888, 1902, 1921, 1981

12. **SR** : CM, *IV*, 1878, 1888, 1902, 1921, 1981

13. Not in OT1

14. **SR** : (*TS*), (1851), CM, *IV*, 1878, 1888, 1902, 1921, 1981

15. *IV* "my", followed by 1878 / 1888 "mine", followed by 1902, 1921, 1981

16. **Scribe undetermined** : (*TS*), (1851), CM, *IV*, 1878, 1888, 1902, 1921, 1981

17. "none other" : (*TS*), (1851), CM "no", followed by *IV*, 1878, 1888, 1902, 1921, 1981

18. (*TS*), (1851) "besides"

19. OT1 "And"

20. (*TS*), (1851), CM insert "unto", followed by *IV*, 1878, 1888, 1902, 1921, 1981

21. (*TS*), (1851), 1902 omit "as", followed by 1921, 1981

22. **SR** : CM, *IV*, 1878, 1888, 1902, 1921, 1981 / (1851) "were"

23. **SR** : CM, *IV*, 1878, 1888, 1902, 1921, 1981 / (*TS*), (1851) "are"

24. **SR** : not in (*TS*), (1851), CM, *IV*, 1878, 1888, 1902, 1921, 1981

that it was for the space of many hours before ~~Moses~~ <he>[25] did again
Receive his natural strength like unto man and he ~~saith~~ <said>[26] unto him-
self Now for this once[27] I know that man is nothing which thing
I never had supposed [11] But now mine \[28] eyes ~~mine own eyes~~ <have be-
    held God>[29] but not
mine[30] <natural>[31] eyes[32] <but my spiritual>[33] \[34], for mine[35] <natural>[36]
    eyes could not have beheld for I should have
withered and died in his presence But his glory was upon me and I
beheld his face for I was transfigured before him. [12] And now[37] it came
    <to pass>[38]
that when Moses had said these words Behold satan came tempting
him Saying Moses Son of man worship me [13] ~~And it came to~~
~~pass that~~ <but>[39] Moses <lifted up his eyes and>[40] looked upon Satan and
    ~~saith~~ <said>[41] Who art thou for
Behold I am a Son of God in the similitude of his only begotten
and where is thy glory that I should worship thee [14] for behold I could
not look upon God except his glory should come upon me and I

---

25. **SR** : not in (*TS*), (1851), CM, *IV*, 1878, 1888, 1902, 1921, 1981

26. **SR** : (1851), CM, *IV*, 1878, 1888, 1902, 1921, 1981

27. (*TS*), (1851), CM "cause", followed by *IV*, 1878, 1888, 1902, 1921, 1981

28. 1902 inserts "own", followed by 1921, 1981

29. **SR** : CM, *IV*, 1878, 1888, 1902, 1921, 1981

30. 1878 "my", followed by 1888, 1902, 1921, 1981

31. **SR** : CM, *IV*, 1878, 1888, 1902, 1921, 1981

32. CM omits "eyes", followed by *IV*, 1878, 1888, 1902, 1921, 1981

33. **SR** : CM, *IV*, 1878, 1888, 1902, 1921, 1981

34. CM inserts "eyes", followed by *IV*, 1878, 1888, 1902, 1921, 1981

35. 1878 "my", followed by 1888, 1902, 1921, 1981

36. **SR** : CM, *IV*, 1878, 1888, 1902, 1921, 1981

37. (*TS*), (1851), 1902 omit "now", followed by 1921, 1981

38. **SR** corrects to OT1 : (*TS*), (1851), CM, *IV*, 1878, 1888, 1902, 1921, 1981

39. **SR** : not in (*TS*), (1851), CM, *IV*, 1878, 1888, 1902, 1921, 1981

40. **SR** : not in (*TS*), (1851), CM, *IV*, 1878, 1888, 1902, 1921, 1981

41. **SR** : (*TS*), (1851), CM, *IV*, 1878, 1888, 1902, 1921, 1981

were <was>[42] transfigured[43] before him but I can look upon thee in the
natural man! is if not is[44] [15] surely blessed be[45] the name of my God

OT2 Page 2 (Moses 1:15–28)

For his spirit hath not altogether withdrawn from me. or else <I say>[46] where
is thy glory for it is blackness[47] unto me and I can[48] Judge between
thee and God for God said unto me, Worship God for him only shalt
thou serve [16] Get thee[49] hence, Satan, deceive me not, for God said
unto me Thou art after the similitude of mine only begotten. [17] and he
also[50] gave unto[51] me commandment[52], when he called unto me
out of the burning bush[53], Saying, call upon God, in the name
of mine only begotten, and worship me. [18] And again, Moses saith
    <said,>[54] I
will not cease to call upon God, I have other[55] things to inquire
of him for his glory has been upon me and it is glory unto me[56]
wherefore I can Judge betwixt <between>[57] him and thee. Depart hence,
    Satan.

---

42. **SR** : not in (*TS*), (1851), CM, *IV*, 1878, 1888, 1902, 1921, 1981

43. (*TS*), (1851), 1902 "strengthened", followed by 1921 / 1981 "transfigured"

44. **JW** or **SR** : OT1 "if not so" / (*TS*), (1851), CM "Is it not so surely?", followed by *IV*,
     1878, 1888, 1902, 1921, 1981

45. (*TS*), (1851) "is"

46. **SR** : not in (*TS*), (1851), CM, *IV*, 1878, 1888, 1902, 1921, 1981

47. (*TS*), (1851), CM "darkness", followed by *IV*, 1878, 1888, 1902, 1921, 1981

48. (*TS*), (1851) "am"

49. (*TS*), (1851) "thou"

50. (1851) "likewise"

51. (*TS*), 1902 omit "unto", followed by 1921, 1981

52. (*TS*), (1851), 1902 "commandments", followed by 1921, 1981

53. (*TS*), (1851) ""burning bush""

54. **SR** : (*TS*), (1851), CM, *IV*, 1878, 1888, 1902, 1921, 1981

55. (*TS*), (1851) "these"

56. (*TS*), (1851), 1902 omit "and it is glory unto me", followed by 1921, 1981

57. **SR** : (*TS*), (1851), CM, *IV*, 1878, 1888, 1902, 1921, 1981

[19] And now when Moses had said these words Satan cried with a
loud voice and wrent[58] upon the Earth, and commanded, saying, I am
the only begotten, worship me. [20] And it came to pass that Moses
began to fear exceedingly, and as he began to fear, he saw the bitterness of Hell, Nevertheless, calling upon God he received strength
and he commanded Saying, Depart hence[59], Satan, for this one God
only will I worship, which is the God of glory. [21] And now Satan
began to tremble, and the Earth shook, \[60] and Moses received[61] strength
<and>[62] called upon God ~~saying~~[63] in the name of ~~Jesus Christ~~ <his Son[64]
        saying to Satan>[65] depart
hence. ~~Satan~~[66] [22] and[67] it came to pass that Satan cried with a loud
voice with weeping and wailing[68] and gnashing of teeth, and \[69] departed
        hence

---

58. (*TS*), (1851), CM "went", followed by *IV* / 1878 "rent", followed by 1888, 1902,
    1921 / 1981 "ranted"

59. (*TS*), (1851), 1902 "from me", followed by 1921, 1981

60. Joseph Smith's revision of the following sentence reads (modern punctuation added):
    "And Moses received strength and called upon God in the name of his Son, saying to
    Satan: Depart hence." / (*TS*), (1851) ". . . called upon God, saying, in the name of
    Jesus Christ, depart hence Satan." / CM ". . . called upon God in the name of Jesus
    Christ, saying to Satan, Depart Hence." / *IV*, 1878, 1888 ". . . called upon God in
    the name of the Only Begotten, saying to Satan, Depart hence." / 1902 ". . . called
    upon God, saying: In the name of the Only Begotten, depart hence, Satan.", followed
    by 1921, 1981

61. OT1 "receiving"

62. **SR** : (*TS*), (1851), CM, *IV*, 1878, 1888, 1902, 1921, 1981

63. **SR** : CM, *IV*, 1878, 1888 / (*TS*), (1851), 1902 insert "saying", followed by 1921,
    1981

64. "in the name of his Son" : (*TS*), (1851), CM "in the name of Jesus Christ" / *IV* "in
    the name of the Only Begotten", followed by 1878, 1888, 1902, 1921, 1981

65. **SR**

66. **SR** : CM, *IV*, 1878, 1888 / (*TS*), (1851), 1902 insert "Satan", followed by 1921,
    1981

67. OT1 "And"

68. (*TS*), (1851) omit "and wailing"

69. 1902 inserts "he", followed by 1921, 1981

yea[70] from the presence of Moses that he beheld him not. [23] And
now of this thing Moses bore record but because of wickedness
it is not had among the Children of men. [24] And it came to pass
that when Satan had departed from the presence of Moses ~~he~~ <that
     Moses>[71] lifted
up his eyes unto Heaven being filled with the Holy Ghost
which beareth record of the Father and the son; [25] and calling upon[72] the
name of God, he beheld again[73] his glory \[74], for it ~~was~~ <rested>[75] upon him
and he heard a voice, saying, Blessed art thou Moses, for I, the almigh-
ty have chosen thee, And thou shalt[76] be made stronger than the[77]
many Waters, for they shall obey thy command even[78] as ~~if thou~~
~~wert God~~ <my commandments>[79]. [26] And lo I am with thee[80] even
     unto[81] the end of thy days
for thou shalt deliver my people from bondage, even Israel my
chosen. [27] And it came to pass, as the[82] voice was still speaking, he[83]
cast his eyes and beheld[84] the Earth yea even all[85] the face[86] of it

---

70. (*TS*), (1851), 1902 "even", followed by 1921, 1981

71. **SR** : CM, *IV*, 1878, 1888, 1902, 1921, 1981

72. (*TS*) "on"

73. (*TS*), (1851), 1902 omit "again", followed by 1921, 1981

74. (*TS*), (1851), 1902 insert "again", followed by 1921, 1981

75. **SR** : CM, *IV*, 1878, 1888 / (*TS*), (1851), 1902 "was", followed by 1921, 1981

76. (*TS*) "shall"

77. (*TS*), (1851), CM omit "the", followed by *IV*, 1878, 1888, 1902, 1921, 1981

78. (*TS*), (1851), 1902 omit "even", followed by 1921, 1981

79. **SR** : not in (*TS*), (1851), CM, *IV*, 1878, 1888, 1902, 1921, 1981

80. OT1 "you"

81. OT1 "to"

82. (*TS*), (1851) "Moses'"

83. 1902 "Moses", followed by 1921, 1981

84. (*TS*) "behold"

85. OT1 "all all"

86. 1902 omits "the face", followed by 1921, 1981

and[87] there was not a particle of it which he did not behold, discerning[88]
it by the spirit of God. [28] and he beheld also the Inhabitants thereof
and there was not a soul which he beheld not, and he discerned them

OT2 Page 3 (Moses 1:28–42)

by the spirit of God, and their numbers were great, even as[89] numberless as the sand upon the Sea shore. [29] and he beheld many lands
and each land was called Earth, and there were inhabitants on[90] the face
    there-
of. [30] And it came to pass that Moses called upon God saying ~~tell~~
    <show>[91]
me I pray thee why these things are so and by ~~what~~ <whom>[92] thou madest
them [31] and Behold, the glory of God[93] was upon Moses so[94] that moses
    stood
in the presence of God and he[95] talked with him[96] face to face. and the
Lord God said unto Moses, For mine own purpose have I made
these things, here is wisdom, and it remaineth in me, [32] And by the
word of my power, have I created them, which is mine[97] only begotten
Son, who is[98] full of grace and truth. [33] And worlds without number
have I created, and[99] I also created them for mine own purpose, and by
the same[100] I created them, which is mine only begotten, [34] And the first

---

87. (*TS*), (1851) omit "and"

88. (*TS*), (1851) "descrying"

89. (*TS*), (1851), 1902 omit "as", followed by 1921, 1981

90. OT1 "upon"

91. **SR** : not in (*TS*), (1851), CM, *IV*, 1878, 1888, 1902, 1921, 1981

92. **SR** : not in (*TS*), (1851), CM, *IV*, 1878, 1888, 1902, 1921, 1981

93. 1902 "the Lord", followed by 1921, 1981

94. Not in OT1

95. 1902 omits "he", followed by 1921, 1981

96. (*TS*), (1851) "Moses"

97. 1888 "my" / 1902 "mine", followed by 1921, 1981

98. "who is" : not in OT1

99. 1888 "and and"

100. (*TS*), (1851), CM "Son", followed by *IV*, 1878, 1888, 1902, 1921, 1981

man of all men have I called Adam, which is many, [35] but
only an account of this Earth, and the inhabitants thereof give I
unto you. For Behold, there are many Worlds which[101] have
passed away by the word[102] of my power, and there are many also[103]
which[104] now stand, and numberless[105] are they unto man; but
all things are numbered unto me. For they are mine and I know
them. [36] And it came to pass that Moses spake unto the Lord
saying, Be merciful unto thy servant, O God, and tell me concerning this Earth and the inhabitants thereof and also the Heavens and
then thy Servant will be content. [37] \\[106] And the Lord God ~~said~~
    <spake>[107] unto
Moses ~~Saying~~ <of>[108] the Heavens <saying>[109] ~~there~~ <these>[110] are many,
    and they cannot be numbered
unto man but they are numbered unto me for they are mine [38] and as
one Earth shall pass away and the Heavens thereof even so shall
another come And there is no end to my works neither \\[111] my words
[39] for[112] Behold[113] this is my work ~~to~~ <and>[114] my glory to ~~the~~ <bring to

---

101.   1888 "that", followed by 1902, 1921, 1981

102.   (*TS*), (1851) "words"

103.   (*TS*), (1851), 1902 omit "also", followed by 1921, 1981

104.   1902 "that", followed by 1921, 1981

105.   (*TS*), (1851), 1902 "innumerable", followed by 1921, 1981

106.   Joseph Smith's revision of the following sentence reads (modern punctuation added):
     "And the Lord God spake unto Moses of the heavens, saying: These are many . . ." /
     (*TS*), (1851), CM "And the Lord God spake unto Moses saying, The heavens, they
     are many . . .", followed by *IV*, 1878, 1888, 1902, 1921, 1981

107.   SR corrects to OT1 : (*TS*), (1851), CM, *IV*, 1878, 1888, 1902, 1921, 1981

108.   SR : not in (*TS*), (1851), CM, *IV*, 1878, 1888, 1902, 1921, 1981

109.   SR : not in (*TS*), (1851), CM, *IV*, 1878, 1888, 1902, 1921, 1981

110.   SR : (*TS*), (1851), CM "they", followed by *IV*, 1878, 1888, 1902, 1921, 1981

111.   (*TS*), (1851), CM insert "to", followed by *IV*, 1878, 1888, 1902, 1921, 1981

112.   (*TS*), (1851) omit "for"

113.   CM omits "behold", followed by *IV*, 1878, 1888 / 1902 inserts "behold", followed
     by 1921, 1981

114.   SR : CM, *IV*, 1878, 1888, 1902, 1921, 1981

pass the>[115] immortality and \[116]

eternal life of man. [40] And now, Moses, my Son, I will speak unto

you[117] concerning this Earth upon which ~~thou~~ <you>[118] standest[119], and
    ~~thou~~ <you>[120]

~~shalt~~ <shall>[121] write the[122] things which I shall speak. [41] And in a day when

the children of men shall esteem my words as naught, and take

many of them from the Book which ~~thou~~ <you>[123] ~~shalt~~ <shall>[124] write,
    Behold, I

will raise up another like unto ~~thee~~ <you,>[125] and they shall be had again

among the Children of men, \[126] Among even[127] as many as shall

believe. [42] These[128] words were[129] spoken unto Moses in the Mo-

unt, the name of which shall not be known among the Children

of men. ~~and now they are also~~[130] ~~spoken unto you show them~~

~~not unto any except them that believe~~ <until I command you>[131] ~~amen~~[132]

---

115. **SR** : CM, *IV*, 1878, 1888, 1902, 1921, 1981

116. OT1 "the"

117. (1851), 1902 "thee", followed by 1921, 1981

118. **SR** : CM, *IV*, 1878, 1888 / (*TS*), (1851), 1902 "thou", followed by 1921, 1981

119. **SR** : CM, *IV*, 1878, 1888 / (*TS*), (1851), 1902 "standest", followed by 1921, 1981

120. **SR** : CM, *IV*, 1878, 1888 / (*TS*), (1851), 1902 "thou", followed by 1921, 1981

121. **SR** : (1851), CM, *IV*, 1878, 1888 / (*TS*), 1902 "shalt", followed by 1921, 1981

122. (1851) "these"

123. **SR** : CM, *IV*, 1878, 1888 / (*TS*), (1851), 1902 "thou", followed by 1921, 1981

124. **SR** : CM, *IV*, 1878, 1888 / (*TS*), (1851), 1902 "shalt", followed by 1921, 1981

125. **SR** : CM, *IV*, 1878, 1888 / (*TS*), (1851), 1902 "thee", followed by 1921, 1981

126. (*TS*), (1851) "among as many as shall believe those words were spoken unto Moses in the Mount"

127. (*TS*), (1851), 1902 omit "even", followed by 1921, 1981

128. (*TS*), (1851) "those"

129. OT1 "was"

130. (*TS*), (1851), CM omit "also", followed by *IV*, 1878, 1888, 1902, 1921, 1981

131. Insertion probably **SR** : not in 1902, 1921, 1981

132. Entire strikeout **SR** : (*TS*), (1851), CM "And now they are spoken unto you. Amen", followed by *IV*, 1878, 1888 / 1902 "And now they are spoken unto you. Show them not unto any except them that believe. Even so. Amen", followed by 1921, 1981 / 1921 places all of verse 42 in parentheses, followed by 1981

MOSES 2

OT2 Page 4 (Moses 2:1–16)

[1] And it came to pass, that the Lord spake unto Moses, saying,
Behold, I reveal unto you concerning this Heaven and this Earth; write
the words which I speak, I am the beginning and the end, the Almighty
   God.
By mine only begotten I created these things. yea, in the beginning
I created the Heaven, and the Earth upon which thou standest. [2] and the
Earth was without form, and void. And I caused[1] darkness to come up[2] upon
the face of the deep. and my spirit moved upon the face of the
water[3]; for I am God. [3] and I, God, said, Let there be light, and there was
light. [4] and I, God, saw the light, and that[4] light was Good. and I, God,
   divided
the light from the darkness. [5] and I, God, called the light day, and the
darkness I called night. and this I done[5] <did>[6] by the word[7] of my power.
   and
it was done as I spake. and the evening and the morning were the first
day. [6] And again, I, God, said, Let there be a firmament in the midst

---

1. (1851) "created"
2. (1851) omits "up"
3. OT1 "waters", followed by (1851)
4. OT1 "the", followed by (1851)
5. (1851), CM omit "done", followed by *IV,* 1878, 1888, 1902, 1921, 1981
6. **Scribe undetermined** : (1851), CM, *IV,* 1878, 1888, 1902, 1921, 1981
7. OT1 "Word"

of the water[8]; and it was so, even as I spake. And I said, Let it divide
the waters from the waters; and it was done. [7] and I, God, made the
firmament, and divided the waters; yea the great waters, under
the firmament, from the waters which were above the firmament; and it was so, even as I spake. [8] and[9] I, God, called the firmament
Heaven. and the evening and the[10] morning were the Second day. [9] And I,
God, said, Let the waters[11] under the[12] Heaven be gathered together
unto[13] one place; and it was so. and I, God, said, Let there be dry Land,
and it was so. [10] and I, God, called the dry land Earth; and the gathering
together
of the waters called I the[14] Sea<s>[15]. And I, God, saw that all things that[16]
I had made were good. [11] And I, God, said, Let the Earth bring forth
grass;
the herb yielding seed; the fruit tree yielding fruit after his
kind; and the tree yielding fruit, whose seed should be in itself,
upon the Earth; and it was so, even as I spake. [12] and the Earth brought
forth grass; every herb yielding seed after his kind; and the tree
yielding fruit, whose seed should be in itself, after his[17] kind.
And I, God, saw that all things which I had made were good. [13] and
the even-
ing and the morning were the third day. [14] and I, God, said, Let
<there>[18] be lights

---

8. OT1 "waters", followed by (1851)

9. OT1 "And"

10. 1888 omits "the" / 1902 inserts "the", followed by 1921, 1981

11. 1888 "water", followed by 1902 / 1921 "waters", followed by 1981

12. (1851) omits "the"

13. (1851) "into"

14. **Scribe undetermined**, post-1845 : deletion not in (1851), CM, *IV*, 1878, 1888, 1902, 1921, 1981

15. **Scribe undetermined**, post-1845, corrects to OT1 : not in CM, *IV*, 1878, 1888, 1902, 1921, 1981

16. OT1 "which", followed by CM, *IV*, 1878, 1888, 1902, 1921, 1981

17. OT1 "its"

18. **SR** corrects to OT1 : (1851), CM, *IV*, 1878, 1888, 1902, 1921, 1981

in the firmament of the[19] Heaven, to divide the day from the night;
and let them be for signs, and for seasons, and for days and for years; [15]
    and let
them be for lights in the firmament of the Heaven, to give light
upon the Earth; and it was so. [16] and I, God, made two great lights; the
greater light to rule the day, and the lesser light to rule the night;
and the greater light was the sun, and the lesser light was the moon.

OT2 Page 5 (Moses 2:16–31)

And the stars also[20] ~~was~~ <were>[21] made, even according to my word; [17]
    and I,
God, set them in the firmament of the[22] Heaven, to give light upon
the Earth. [18] and the Sun to rule over the day, and the Moon to rule over
the night, and to divide the light from the darkness. and I God saw
that all things which I had[23] made were good. [19] and the evening and the
morning were the fourth day. [20] and I, God, said, Let the waters bring
forth abundantly, the[24] moving creature that hath life, and fowl
which may fly above the Earth[25], in the open firmament of Heaven.
[21] and I, God, created great whales; and every living creature that moveth,
which the water<s>[26] brought forth abundantly, after their kind; and
every winged fowl, after his kind; and I, God, saw that all things
which I had[27] created[28] were good; [22] and I, God, blessed them, saying, be
fruitful, and multiply, and fill the waters in the Seas[29], and let fowl

---

19. 1888 omits "the" / 1902 inserts "the", followed by 1921, 1981

20. (1851) omits "also"

21. **SR** : (1851), CM, *IV*, 1878, 1888, 1902, 1921, 1981

22. (1851), 1888 omit "the" / 1902 inserts "the", followed by 1921, 1981

23. Not in OT1

24. (1851) "every"

25. (1851) omits "above the Earth"

26. **Scribe undetermined** corrects to OT1 : (1851), CM, *IV*, 1878, 1888, 1902, 1921, 1981

27. 1888 omits "had" / 1902 inserts "had", followed by 1921, 1981

28. (1851) "made"

29. **SR** : CM, *IV*, 1878, 1888, 1902, 1921, 1981

multiply in the Earth; [23] and the evening and the morning were the
fifth day. [24] and I, God, said, Let the Earth bring forth the living
creature, after his kind; cattle, and creeping things[30], and beasts[31] of the
    Earth, after ~~his~~ \<their\>[32] ~~kinds~~[33];
and it was so. [25] and I, God, made the beasts[34] of the Earth, after ~~his~~
    \<their\>[35] kind;
and cattle after their kind; and every thing[36] which creepeth upon the Earth
after his kind. and I, God, saw that all these things were good. [26] and I[37],
\[38] God, said, unto mine[39] Only Begotten, which[40] was with me[41] from
the beginning, Let us make man in our \[42] image, after our
likeness; and it was so[43]. and I[44], \[45] God, said Let them have dominion over
the fishes[46] of the Sea, and over the fowl[47] of the Air, and over the
Cattle, and over all the Earth, and over every creeping thing that
creepeth[48] upon the Earth. [27] and[49] I[50], God, created man in mine[51]

---

30. OT1 "thing"
31. OT1 "beast"
32. **SR** : (1851), CM, *IV*, 1878, 1888, 1902, 1921, 1981
33. **SR** corrects to OT1 / CM, *IV*, 1878, 1888, 1902, 1921, 1981
34. OT1 "beast"
35. **SR** : (1851), CM, *IV*, 1878, 1888, 1902, 1921, 1981
36. "every thing" : *IV* "everything" / 1878 "every thing" / 1888 "everything",
    followed by 1902, 1921, 1981
37. (LF) omits "I"
38. (LF) inserts "the Lord"
39. (LF) "the"
40. (LF) "who"
41. (LF) "him"
42. (1851) inserts "own"
43. (LF) "done"
44. (LF) omits "I"
45. (LF) inserts "the Lord"
46. OT1 "fish", followed by (LF)
47. (1851) "fowls"
48. (LF) "creeps"
49. OT1 "So", followed by (LF)
50. (LF) omits "I"
51. (LF) "his"

own image; in the image of mine[52] Only Begotten created
I[53] him; male and female created I[54] them. [28] and I[55], God, blessed them
and I[56] God[57] said unto them, Be fruitful, and multiply, and replenish
the Earth, and subdue it; and have dominion over the fish[58] of
the Sea, and over the fowl of the Air, and over every living thing
that moveth[59] upon the Earth. [29] and I[60], \[61] God, said unto man, Behold
I have given you every herb bearing Seed, which is upon the face
of all the Earth; and every tree in the which shall be[62] the
fruit of a tree, yielding seed; to you it shall be for meat.
[30] and to every beast of the Earth, and to every fowl of the Air, and
to every thing[63] that creepeth upon the Earth, wherein I grant
life, there shall be given every clean herb for meat; and it
was so, even as I spake. [31] and I, God, saw every thing[64] that I had
made, and Behold all things which I had made were very good

OT2 Page 6 (Moses 2:31–3:12)

And the evening and the morning were the sixth day.

---

52. (LF) "the"
53. (LF) "he"
54. (LF) "he"
55. (LF) omits "I"
56. (LF) omits "I"
57. CM omits "I God", followed by *IV*, 1878, 1888, 1902, 1921, 1981
58. (1851) "fishes"
59. (LF) "moves"
60. (LF) omits "I"
61. (LF) inserts "the Lord"
62. "shall be" : (LF) "is"
63. "every thing" : *IV* "everything" / 1878 "every thing" / 1888 "everything" / 1902 "every thing" / 1921 "everything", followed by 1981
64. "every thing" : *IV* "everything", followed by 1878, 1888, 1902, 1921, 1981

MOSES 3

[1] Thus the Heaven and the Earth were finished, and all the host of them. [2] and on the Seventh day I God ended my work and all things which I had made and I rested on the Seventh day from all my work and all things which I had made were finished. And I <God>[1] saw that they were good. [3] And I, God, blessed the seventh day, and

Sanctified it, because that in it[2] I had rested from all my work which I God had created and made. [4] And now Behold I say unto you that these are the generations of the Heaven and of the Earth when they were created in the day that I the Lord God made the Heaven and the Earth [5] and every plant of the field before it was in the Earth and every herb of the field before it grew, for I the lord God Created all things of which I have spoken Spiritually, before they were naturally upon the face of the Earth, For[3] I the Lord God had not caused it to rain upon the face of the Earth. and I the Lord God[4] had created all the Children of men and not yet a man to till the ground, for in Heaven created I them. And there was not yet flesh upon the Earth neither in the water neither in the air [6] but I the Lord God Spake and there went up a mist from the Earth and

---

1. **SR** : (1851), CM, *IV*, 1878, 1888, 1902, 1921, 1981
2. (1851) omits "that in it"
3. (1851) "And"
4. (1851) omits "had not caused . . . the Lord God"

watered the whole face of the ground [7] and I the Lord God formed,
man from the dust of the ground and breathed into his nostrils
the breath of life, and man became a living soul the first flesh
upon the Earth the first man also. nevertheless all things were
before created, but Spiritually were they created and made according to my word, [8] and I the Lord God planted a Garden eastward
in Eden and there I put the man whom I had formed.
[9] And out of the ground made[5] I the Lord God \\[6] to grow \\[7] every
tree naturally[8] that is pleasant to the sight of man and man
could behold it and ~~they~~ <it>[9] became also a living soul for[10] it was
spiritual in the day that I created it for it remaineth in the
sphere <in>[11] which I <God>[12] created it \\[13] yea, even all things which I
prepared for the use of man and man saw that it was good for
food. and I the Lord God ~~placed~~ <planted>[14] the tree of life also in the midst
of the garden and also the tree of knowledge of good and evil
[10] and <I the Lord God caused>[15] a river ~~went~~ <to go>[16] out of Eden to
        water the garden and from thence
it was parted and became into four heads. [11] and I the Lord God
called the name of the first Pison and it compasseth the whole
land of Havilah[17] where ~~there were~~[18] <I the Lord>[19] \\[20] created much gold
        [12] and the

---

5. (1851) omits "made"

6. (1851) inserts "made"

7. (1851) inserts "naturally"

8. (1851) omits "naturally"

9. **SR** : CM, *IV*, 1878, 1888, 1902, 1921, 1981

10. (1851) omits "for"

11. **SR** : CM, *IV*, 1878, 1888, 1902, 1921, 1981

12. **SR** : (1851), CM, *IV*, 1878, 1888, 1902, 1921, 1981

13. (1851) inserts "in"

14. **SR** : CM, *IV*, 1878, 1888, 1902, 1921, 1981

15. **SR** : CM, *IV*, 1878, 1888, 1902, 1921, 1981

16. **SR** : CM, *IV*, 1878, 1888, 1902, 1921, 1981

17. 1888 "Hivilah" / 1902 "Havilah", followed by 1902, 1921, 1981

18. (1851) "was"

19. **SR** : CM, *IV*, 1878, 1888, 1902, 1921, 1981

20. 1902 inserts "God", followed by 1921, 1981

OT2 Page 7 (Moses 3:12–4:3)

Gold of that land was good and there was bdellium and the Onyx stone
[13] And the name of the Second River was called Gihon[21] the same
~~was it~~[22] that compasseth[23] the whole land of Ethiopia [14] And the
name of the third River[24] was Hiddekel that ~~was it~~[25] which[26] goeth
towards[27] the East of Assyria And the fourth River was \[28] Euphra-
tes. [15] And I[29] the Lord God took the man and put him into the
Garden of Eden to dress it and to keep it [16] and I[30] the Lord God com-
manded the man saying, Of every tree of the garden thou[31]
mayest[32] freely eat, [17] but of the tree of the[33] knowledge of good
and evil thou[34] shalt[35] not eat of it, \[36] nevertheless, thou[37] mayest[38] choose
for thyself[39], for it is given unto thee[40]. But remember, that

---

21. (1851) "Ghihon"
22. **SR** : CM, *IV*, 1878, 1888, 1902, 1921, 1981
23. (1851) "compassed"
24. (1851) omits "River"
25. **SR** : CM, *IV*, 1878, 1888, 1902, 1921, 1981
26. (1851) "that"
27. CM "toward", followed by *IV* / 1878 "towards", followed by 1888 / 1902 "toward", followed by 1921, 1981
28. 1888 inserts "the", followed by 1902, 1921, 1981
29. (*LF*) omits "I"
30. (*LF*) omits "I"
31. (*LF*) "you"
32. (*LF*) "may"
33. (1851) omits "the"
34. (*LF*) "you"
35. (*LF*) "shall"
36. (*LF*) inserts "neither shall you touch it"
37. (*LF*) "you"
38. (*LF*) "may"
39. (*LF*) "yourself"
40. (*LF*) "you"

I forbid it[41], for in the day that[42] thou[43] eatest[44] thereof thou[45] shalt[46] surely die. [18] And I the Lord God said unto mine only Begotten that
it was not good that the man should be alone Wherefore I will make
an[47] help meet[48] for him. [19] and out of the ground I[49] the Lord God
    formed
every beast of the field and every fowl of the air and commanded that
they should ~~be brought~~ <come>[50] unto Adam to see what he would call
    them
and they were also living souls ~~and it was~~ <for I, God,>[51] breathed into
    them the breath
of life and <commanded that>[52] whatsoever[53] Adam called every living
    creature that ~~was~~ <should be>[54]
the name thereof. [20] and Adam gave names to all cattle and to the fowl
of the air and to every beast of the field but <as>[55] for Adam there
was not found an[56] help meet[57] for him. [21] and I, the Lord God, caus-

---

41. (1851) omits "it"

42. *IV* omits "that", followed by 1878, 1888, 1902, 1921, 1981

43. (*LF*) "you"

44. (*LF*) "eat"

45. (*LF*) "you"

46. (*LF*) "shall"

47. OT1 "a", followed by (1851)

48. "help meet" : 1878 "help-meet" / 1888 "helpmeet", followed by 1902 / 1921 "help meet", followed by 1981

49. (*LF*) omits "I"

50. **SR** : CM, *IV*, 1878, 1888, 1902, 1921, 1981

51. **SR** : CM, *IV*, 1878, 1888, 1902, 1921, 1981

52. **SR** : CM, *IV*, 1878, 1888, 1902, 1921, 1981

53. (*LF*) "whatever"

54. **SR** : CM, *IV*, 1878, 1888, 1902, 1921, 1981

55. **SR** : CM, *IV*, 1878, 1888, 1902, 1921, 1981

56. OT1 "a", followed by (1851)

57. "help meet" : 1878 "help-meet" / 1888 "helpmeet", followed by 1902 / 1921 "help meet", followed by 1981

ed a deep sleep to fall[58] upon Adam, and he slept, and I took one of his ribs and closed up the flesh in the stead thereof, [22] and the rib which I, the Lord God had taken from man, made I a woman, and brought her unto the man. [23] and Adam said, This I know now is bone of my bones and flesh of my flesh, she shall be called woman, because she was taken out of man. [24] Therefore shall a man leave his father and \\[59] mother and shall[60] cleave unto his wife and they \\[61] shall be one flesh. [25] and they were both naked, the man and his wife, and were not ashamed.

---

58. (1851) "come"
59. OT1 "his", followed by CM, *IV*, 1878, 1888, 1902, 1921, 1981
60. (1851) omits "shall"
61. (1851) inserts "twain"

MOSES 4

[1] And I the Lord God spake unto Moses saying, That Satan
whom thou hast commanded in the name of mine only begotten
is the same which was from the beginning, and he came before me
saying, Behold \\[1] I[2], send me, I will be thy Son, and I will redeem all
mankind, that one soul shall not be lost; and surely, I will do
it; Wherefore, give me thine honor. [2] But, behold; my beloved
Son, which was my beloved and chosen from the beginning, ~~saith~~ <said>[3]
   unto me;
Father, thy will be done, and the glory be thine forever[4]. [3] Wherefore,
because that satan rebelled against me, and sought to destroy the

OT2 Page 8 (Moses 4:3–20)

Agency of man, which I, the Lord God had given him; and also
that I should give unto him mine own power; by the power
of mine only begotten, I caused that he should be cast down,
[4] and he became Satan; yea, even the Devil, the father of all lies,
to deceive, and to blind men, and to lead them captive at his will,
even as many as would not hearken unto my voice. [5] and now
the Serpent was more subtle then any beast of the field which
I the Lord God had made [6] and Satan put it into the heart of

---

1. 1902 inserts "here am", followed by 1921, 1981
2. (1851) "me"
3. **SR** : (1851), CM, *IV*, 1878, 1888, 1902, 1921, 1981
4. (1851) "for ever"

the serpent \\[5] for he had drew[6] away many after him; \\[7] and he
sought also to beguile Eve, for he knew not the mind of
God; Wherefore, he sought[8] to destroy the world, [7] ~~yea~~[9] and he said
unto the woman, yea, hath God said, ye shall not eat of
every tree of the garden. \\[10] and he spake by the mouth of the
Serpent \\[11] [8] <And the woman said unto the Serpent, we may eat of the
    fruit of the trees of the garden>[12] [9] but, of the fruit of the tree
    which thou beholdest in the midst of
the garden, God hath said ye shall not eat of it neither
shall ye touch[13] it lest ye die [10] <And the serpent said unto the woman
    ye shall[14] not surely die>[15] [11] for God doth know that in
the day ye eat thereof then your eyes shall be opened and
ye shall be as Gods knowing good and evil. [12] and when the woman
saw that the tree was good for food, and that it became
pleasant to the eyes[16], and a tree to be desired to make her
wise, she took of the fruit thereof, and did eat; and gave also[17] unto
her husband with her, and he did eat; [13] and the eyes of them both were
opened, and they knew that they had been naked; and they sewed fig leaves[18]
together and made themselves aprons[19]. [14] and they[20] heard the voice of the
Lord God, <~~as he was~~ <as they were>>[21] walking in the garden in the cool

---

5. (1851), 1878 insert "(", followed by 1888, 1902, 1921, 1981
6. (1851), CM "drawn", followed by *IV*, 1878, 1888, 1902, 1921, 1981
7. (1851), 1878 insert ")", followed by 1888, 1902, 1921, 1981
8. OT1 "thought"
9. Probably **SR** : CM, *IV*, 1878, 1888, 1902, 1921, 1981
10. (1851), 1878 insert "(", followed by 1888, 1902, 1921, 1981
11. (1851), 1878 insert ")", followed by 1888, 1902, 1921, 1981
12. **SR** : CM, *IV*, 1878, 1888, 1902, 1921, 1981
13. (1851) "taste"
14. 1878 "shalt", followed by 1888 / 1902 "shall", followed by 1921, 1981
15. **SR** : CM, *IV*, 1878, 1888, 1902, 1921, 1981
16. (1851) "eye"
17. "gave also" : 1888 "also gave", followed by 1902, 1921, 1981
18. "fig leaves" : 1921 "fig-leaves", followed by 1981
19. (1851) omits "and they sewed . . . themselves aprons"
20. (1851) omits "sewed fig leaves . . . and they"
21. **SR** / OT1 "<as they were>" : probably **JS**, followed by (LF), (1851), CM, *IV*, 1878,

of[22] the day and Adam

and his wife ~~hid~~ \<went to hide\>[23] themselves from the presence of I[24] the
Lord God

amongst[25] the trees of the garden [15] and I[26] the Lord God called unto
Adam and said unto him Where goest thou[27] [16] and he said I heard
thy[28] voice in the garden and I was afraid because I beheld that I was naked
and I hid myself. [17] and I[29] the Lord God said unto Adam who told
thee[30] that[31] thou[32] wast[33] naked hast[34] thou[35] eaten of the tree whereof
I commanded[36] thee[37] that thou[38] shouldest[39] not eat if so thou[40]

1888, 1902, 1921, 1981. Some small insertions in OT1, page 7, appear to be in the
handwriting of Joseph Smith. They were made sometime after March–April 1831
(when OT2 was transcribed) and most likely before July 1832 (when work resumed
on Genesis after the completion of the New Testament). These insertions were probably made before the Prophet decided that OT2 would be the manuscript on which
further changes in the Genesis translation would be made.

22. OT1 "of of"

23. **SR** : CM, *IV*, 1878, 1888, 1902, 1921, 1981

24. **SR** : CM, *IV*, 1878, 1888, 1902, 1921, 1981

25. (LF), (1851) "among"

26. (LF), (1851) omit "I"

27. "goest thou" : (LF), (1851) "are you going"

28. (LF), (1851) "your"

29. (LF), (1851) omit "I"

30. (LF), (1851) "you"

31. 1878 omits "that", followed by 1888, 1902, 1921, 1981

32. (LF), (1851) "you"

33. (LF), (1851) "were"

34. (LF), (1851) "have"

35. (LF), (1851) "you"

36. (LF), (1851) "told"

37. (LF), (1851) "you"

38. (LF), (1851) "you"

39. OT1 "shouldst", followed by CM, *IV*, 1878, 1888, 1902, 1921, 1981 / (LF), (1851)
"should"

40. (LF), (1851) "you"

should<est>[41]

surely die [18] and the man said, the woman whom[42] thou[43] gavest[44] me
and saidest <unto her>[45] remain with thee[46] she[47] gave me of the \[48] tree
    and I
did eat. [19] and I[49], the Lord God, said unto the woman, what is
this thing[50] which thou[51] hast[52] done. and[53] the woman said, the
Serpent beguiled me, and I did eat. [20] \[54] and \[55] <I>[56] the Lord God
    said unto the
serpent, because thou hast done this, thou shalt be cursed
above all cattle, and above every beast of the field; upon thy

OT2 Page 9 (Moses 4:20–5:1)

Belly shalt thou go, and dust shalt thou eat all the days of thy
life; [21] and I will put enmity between thee, and the woman; between

---

41. **Scribe undetermined** / OT1 "shouldst", followed by CM, *IV*, 1878, 1888, 1902, 1921, 1981 / (LF), (1851) "should"
42. 1888 omits "whom", followed by 1902, 1921, 1981
43. (LF), (1851) "you"
44. (LF), (1851) "gave"
45. **Scribe undetermined** / OT1 "~~saidest~~ <commanded that She Should>" : probably JS, followed by (LF), (1851), CM, *IV* / 1878 "commandedst . . . ", followed by 1888, 1902, 1921 / 1981 "commandest . . ."
46. OT1 "~~thee~~ <me>" : probably JS, followed by (LF), (1851), CM, *IV*, 1878, 1888, 1902, 1921, 1981
47. (LF), (1851) omit "she"
48. OT1 "<fruit of the>" : probably JS, followed by (LF), (1851), CM, *IV*, 1878, 1888, 1902, 1921, 1981
49. (LF), (1851) omit "I"
50. (LF), (1851) omit "thing"
51. (LF), (1851) "you"
52. (LF), (1851) "have"
53. Not in OT1
54. (1851) omits verses 20–21
55. OT1 "the"
56. **SR** corrects to OT1 : CM, *IV*, 1878, 1888, 1902, 1921, 1981

thy seed and her seed, and[57] ~~it~~ <he>[58] shall bruise thy head, and thou shalt bruise

his heel. [22] \[59] unto the woman I the Lord God[60] said[61] I will greatly multiply thy[62]

sorrow, and thy[63] conception; in sorrow thou[64] shalt[65] bring

forth children, and thy[66] desire shall be to thy[67] husband, and he shall

rule over thee[68]. [23] and \[69] unto Adam, I, the Lord God, said[70]; because thou[71]

hast[72] hearkened unto the voice of thy[73] wife, and hast[74] eaten of the \[75]

tree \[76] which I commanded thee[77], saying; thou[78] shalt[79] not eat of

it; cursed shall be the ground for thy[80] sake; in sorrow shalt

---

57. Not in OT1
58. **SR** : CM, *IV*, 1878, 1888, 1902, 1921, 1981
59. (LF), (1851) insert "And again, the Lord said"
60. "the Lord God" / not in OT1
61. (LF), (1851) omit "I the Lord God said"
62. (LF), (1851) "your"
63. (LF), (1851) "your"
64. (LF), (1851) "you"
65. (LF), (1851) "shall"
66. (LF), (1851) "your"
67. (LF), (1851) "your"
68. (LF), (1851) "you"
69. (LF), (1851) insert "the Lord God said"
70. (LF), (1851) omit "I, the Lord God, said"
71. (LF), (1851) "you"
72. (LF), (1851) "have"
73. (LF), (1851) "your"
74. (LF), (1851) "have"
75. OT1 "<fruit of the>" : probably **JS**, followed by (LF), (1851), CM, *IV*, 1878, 1888, 1902, 1921, 1981
76. OT1 "of", followed by (LF), (1851), CM, *IV*, 1878, 1888, 1902, 1921, 1981
77. (LF), (1851) "you"
78. (LF), (1851) "you"
79. (LF), (1851) "shall"
80. (LF), (1851) "your"

thou[81] eat of it all the days of thy[82] life; [24] thorns also, and thistles
shall it bring forth to thee[83]; and thou[84] shalt[85] eat the herb of the
field; [25] in[86] the sweat of thy[87] face shalt[88] thou[89] eat bread, until
thou[90] shalt[91] return unto the ground, for thou[92] shalt[93] surely die
for out of it wast thou[94] taken, for dust thou[95] wast[96], and unto dust
shalt thou[97] return. [26] \[98] and[99] Adam called his wife's name Eve, because
she was the mother of all living; for thus have I the Lord God
called the first of all women, which are many. [27] <Unto Adam also, and
to[100] his wife, did I the Lord God, make coats of Skin[101] and clothed
them>[102] [28] And I, the

---

81. "shalt thou" : (LF), (1851) "you shall"

82. (LF), (1851) "your"

83. (LF), (1851) "you"

84. (LF), (1851) "you"

85. (LF), (1851) "shall"

86. OT1 "by", followed by (LF), (1851), CM, *IV*, 1878, 1888, 1902, 1921, 1981

87. (LF), (1851) "your"

88. (LF), (1851) "shall"

89. (LF), (1851) "you"

90. (LF), (1851) "you"

91. (LF), (1851) "shall"

92. (LF), (1851) "you"

93. (LF), (1851) "shall"

94. "wast thou" : (LF), (1851) "you were"

95. (LF), (1851) "you"

96. (LF), (1851) "were"

97. "shalt thou" : (LF), (1851) "you shall"

98. (1851) omits verses 26–32

99. OT1 "And"

100. "also, and to" : CM "and also unto", followed by *IV*, 1878, 1888, 1902, 1921, 1981

101. CM "skins", followed by *IV*, 1878 / 1888 "skin" / 1902 "skins", followed by 1921, 1981

102. **SR** : CM (with modifications), *IV*, 1878, 1888, 1902, 1921, 1981

Lord God, said, unto mine only begotten Behold, the man is
become as one of us, to know good and evil; and now lest he put
forth his hand, and partake also of the tree of life, and eat, and live forever; [29] therefore, I, the lord God, ~~sent~~ <will send>[103] him forth from
the garden of
Eden, to till the ground from whence he was taken; [30] for, as I,
the Lord God, liveth, even so my word<s>[104] cannot[105] return void, for, as
they go forth out of my mouth, they must be fulfilled. [31] so I
drove out the man, and I placed at the east of the garden of Eden,
Cherubims[106] and a flaming Sword, which turned every way, to keep the
way of the tree of life. [32] <(>[107]and these[108] are the words which I spake
unto
my servant Moses and they are true even as I will and I have spoken
them unto you see thou show[109] them unto no man until I
command you except they[110] that believe \[111] amen<)>[112]

---

103. **SR** : CM, *IV*, 1878, 1888, 1902, 1921, 1981

104. **Scribe undetermined** : CM, *IV*, 1878, 1888, 1902, 1921, 1981

105. CM "can not" / *IV* "cannot", followed by 1878, 1888, 1902, 1921, 1981

106. **Scribe undetermined** / CM "cherubims" / *IV* "cherubim", followed by 1878, 1888, 1902, 1921, 1981

107. **Scribe undetermined** : CM, *IV*, 1878, 1888, 1902, 1921, 1981

108. OT1 "those"

109. 1878 "showest", followed by 1888 / 1902 "show", followed by 1921, 1981

110. 1878 "to them", followed by 1888, 1902, 1921, 1981

111. *IV* inserts ")", followed by 1878, 1888, 1902 / 1921 omits ")", followed by 1981

112. **Scribe undetermined** : CM / *IV* omits ")", followed by 1878, 1888, 1902 / 1921 inserts ")", followed by 1981

MOSES 5

[1] ~~For~~[1] <And it came to pass that>[2] after ~~that~~[3] he[4] <I, the Lord God,>[5]
   had ~~been~~[6] driven <them>[7] out \[8] ~~he~~ <that Adam>[9]
began to till the Earth; and to have dominion over all the
beasts of the field, and to eat his bread, by the sweat of the[10]
brow as <I>[11] the lord had commanded him; and Eve also, his wife

OT2 Page 10 (Moses 5:1–14)

Did labor with him. [2] And ~~he~~ <Adam>[12] knew ~~her~~ <his wife,>[13] and
   she bare unto him
Sons and daughters, and they began to multiply, and to replenish the

---

1. (1851) omits "For"
2. **SR** : CM, *IV*, 1878, 1888, 1902, 1921, 1981
3. Deletion not in (*EMS*)
4. (1851) "Adam" / CM omits "he", followed by *IV*, 1878, 1888, 1902, 1921, 1981
5. **SR** : CM, *IV*, 1878, 1888, 1902, 1921, 1981
6. **SR** : CM, *IV*, 1878, 1888, 1902, 1921, 1981
7. **SR** : CM, *IV*, 1878, 1888, 1902, 1921, 1981
8. (1851) inserts "of the garden"
9. **SR** : CM, *IV*, 1878, 1888, 1902, 1921, 1981
10. (LF), CM "his", followed by *IV*, 1878, 1888, 1902, 1921, 1981
11. **SR** : CM, *IV*, 1878, 1888, 1902, 1921, 1981
12. **SR** : CM, *IV*, 1878, 1888, 1902, 1921, 1981
13. **SR** : CM, *IV*, 1878, 1888, 1902, 1921, 1981

Earth, [3] and from that time forth, ~~the~~[14] the sons and daughters
of Adam, began to divide two and two in the land, and to till
the land, and to tend flocks, and they also begat sons and daughters.
[4] and Adam[15] \\[16] called upon the name of the lord, and \\[17] Eve \\[18]
    also, his
wife[19]; and they heard the voice of the lord from the way towards[20]
the garden of Eden, speaking unto them, and they saw him not;
for they were shut out from his presence; [5] and[21] he gave unto
~~him~~ <them>[22] commandment[23], that they should worship the Lord their
God; and should offer the firstlings of their flocks for an offering
unto the Lord. and Adam was obedient unto the commandments[24]
of the Lord[25]. [6] and after many days, an Angel of the Lord appeared
unto Adam, saying why dost[26] thou[27] offer Sacrifices unto the
Lord? and Adam said unto him, I know not, save[28] the Lord

---

14. **Scribe undetermined** corrects to OT1 : (*EMS*), CM, *IV*, 1878, 1888, 1902, 1921, 1981

15. (LF) "he"

16. 1902 inserts "and Eve, his wife", followed by 1921, 1981

17. (LF) inserts "so did"

18. (LF) inserts "his wife"

19. (LF) omits "his wife" / 1902 omits "and Eve also, his wife", followed by 1921, 1981

20. (LF), 1902 "toward", followed by 1921, 1981

21. (LF) "but"

22. **Scribe undetermined** corrects to OT1 : (*EMS*), (LF), (1851), CM, *IV*, 1878, 1888, 1902, 1921, 1981

23. (LF), *IV* "commandments", followed by 1878, 1888, 1902, 1921, 1981

24. (LF), CM "commandment" / *IV* "commandments", followed by 1878, 1888, 1902, 1921, 1981

25. (LF) omits "of the Lord"

26. (LF) "do"

27. (LF) "you"

28. (LF) "but"

commanded me \\[29]. [7] And then the Angel Spake, saying[30], this thing
is a similitude of the Sacrifice of the only begotten of the
Father, which[31] is full of grace and truth, [8] Wherefore[32], thou[33] shalt[34]
do all that thou[35] doest[36], in the name of the Son. and thou[37]
shalt[38] repent, and call upon God, in the[39] name of the Son[40], forever-
more[41]. [9] And[42] in that day, the Holy Ghost[43] fell upon Adam, which[44]
beareth[45] record of the Father and the Son Saying I am ~~Jesus Christ~~
    <the only begotten of the father>[46]
from the beginning hence forth[47] and forever[48]; that as thou hast
fallen, thou mayest be redeemed, and all mankind, even as

---

29. (LF) inserts "to offer sacrifices"
30. "Spake, saying" : (LF) "said unto him"
31. (LF) "who"
32. (LF) "And" / CM "Where fore" / *IV* "Wherefore", followed by 1878, 1888, 1902, 1921, 1981
33. (LF) "you"
34. (LF) "shall"
35. (LF) "you"
36. (LF) "do"
37. (LF) "you"
38. (LF) "shall"
39. (LF) "his"
40. (LF) omits "of the Son"
41. (*EMS*), CM "forever more" / (1851), *IV* "for evermore", followed by 1878, 1888, 1902 / 1921 "forevermore", followed by 1981 / (LF) "forever"
42. (LF) omits "And"
43. (LF) "Spirit"
44. (LF) "and"
45. OT1 "bore", followed by (*EMS*), (LF), (1851)
46. **SR** : CM, *IV*, 1878, 1888, 1902, 1921, 1981
47. "hence forth" : OT1 "henceforth", followed by (1851), CM, *IV*, 1878, 1888, 1902, 1921, 1981
48. (1851), *IV* "for ever", followed by 1878, 1888, 1902 / 1921 "forever", followed by 1981

many as will. [10] and in that day, Adam blessed God and was filled
<del>with the Holy Ghost</del>[49] and began to prophesy concerning all the
families of the Earth
saying[50] Blessed be the name of God, for <because of>[51] my transgression <mine[52] eyes are opened>[53] <del>for</del>
<and>[54] in this life, I shall have Joy, and again, in the[55] flesh, I shall see
God. [11] and eve, his wife heard all these things, and was Glad, saying
were it not for our transgression we should never[56] \[57] had seed,
and should never[58] had[59] known good and evil and the Joy of our
redemption and the eternal life which God giveth unto all the
obedient.
[12] And Adam and Eve blessed the name of God; and they made all
things known unto their sons and their daughters. [13] and satan came
\[60]

among them saying I am also a Son of God; and he com-
manded them, saying, believe <del>it</del>[61] not, and they believed <del>it</del>[62] not;

---

49. **Scribes for insertion and deletion undetermined**

50. (1851) omits "saying"

51. **Scribe undetermined** : CM, *IV*, 1878, 1888, 1902, 1921, 1981

52. CM "my", followed by *IV*, 1878, 1888, 1902, 1921, 1981

53. **Scribe undetermined** : CM, *IV*, 1878, 1888, 1902, 1921, 1981

54. **Scribe undetermined** : CM, *IV*, 1878, 1888, 1902, 1921, 1981

55. OT1 "my", followed by (*EMS*), (1851)

56. "should never" : CM "never should", followed by *IV*, 1878, 1888, 1902, 1921, 1981

57. (1851), CM insert "have", followed by *IV*, 1878, 1888, 1902, 1921, 1981

58. "should never" : CM "never should", followed by *IV*, 1878, 1888, 1902, 1921, 1981

59. (1851), CM "have", followed by *IV*, 1878, 1888, 1902, 1921, 1981

60. OT1 "also", followed by (*EMS*), (1851)

61. **Scribe undetermined** : deletion not in (*EMS*), (1851), CM, *IV*, 1878, 1888, 1902, 1921, 1981

62. **Scribe undetermined** : deletion not in (*EMS*), (1851), CM, *IV*, 1878, 1888, 1902, 1921, 1981

and \[63] loved Satan more than God. and men began from that time
forth, to be carnal, sensual and devilish. [14] and the Lord God, called

OT2 Page 11 (Moses 5:14–30)

upon men, by the Holy Ghost, every where[64], and commanded them,
that they should repent, [15] and as many as believed in the Son, and
  repe-
nted of their sins should be saved; and as many as believed not, and re-
  pented not, should be damned, and the words went forth out of the
mouth of God, in a firm decree. Wherefore, they must be ful-
filled. [16] and Adam \[65] ceased not to call upon God, and Eve also his
wife[66]. and Adam knew Eve, his wife, and she conceived and bare
Cain, and said, I have gotten a man from the Lord; Wherefore,
he may not reject his words; \[67] but, behold, also[68] Cain hearkened
not, Saying, who is the Lord, that I should know him. [17] And she
again conceived, and bare his brother, Abel. and Abel hearkened unto
the voice of the Lord. and Abel was a keeper of sheep, but Cain
was a tiller of the ground. [18] and ~~he~~ <Cain>[69] loved Satan more than
  God.
and Satan commanded him, Saying, make an offering unto the Lord.
[19] And[70] in process of time it came to pass that[71] cain brought of the
fruit of the ground, an offering unto the Lord. [20] and Abel he[72] also
  brought

---

63. CM inserts "they", followed by *IV*, 1878, 1888, 1902, 1921, 1981
64. "every where" : *IV* "everywhere", followed by 1878, 1888, 1902, 1921, 1981
65. 1902 inserts "and Eve, his wife,", followed by 1921, 1981
66. 1902 omits "and Eve also his wife", followed by 1921, 1981
67. (1851) omits "but, behold [verse 16] . . . offering unto the Lord [verse 18]"
68. 1902 omits "also", followed by 1921, 1981
69. **SR** : CM, *IV*, 1878, 1888, 1902, 1921, 1981
70. (LF), (1851) omit "And"
71. (LF), (1851) omit "it came to pass that"
72. (LF), (1851) omit "he"

of the firstlings of his flock and of the fat thereof; and the Lord had re-
spec-
t unto Abel, and to his offering, [21] but unto Cain, and to[73] his offering,
he had not respect. now satan knew this, and it pleased him, and Cain
was very wroth[74] and his countenance fell. [22] and the Lord said unto
Cain, why
art[75] thou[76] wroth[77]? why is thy[78] countenance fallen? [23] if thou[79]
doest[80] well
thou shalt[81] be accepted, and if thou[82] doest[83] not well, sin lieth[84] at the
door, and Satan desireth[85] to have thee[86], and except thou[87] shalt[88]
hearken
unto my commandments, I will deliver thee[89] up; and it shall be unto
thee[90] according to his desire; \[91] and thou shalt rule over him [24] for,
from
this time forth thou shalt be the father of his lies, thou shalt be

---

73. (1851) omits "to"
74. (LF), (1851) "angry"
75. (LF), (1851) "are"
76. (LF), (1851) "you"
77. (LF), (1851) "angry"
78. (LF), (1851) "your"
79. (LF), (1851) "you"
80. (LF), (1851) "do"
81. "thou shalt" : OT1 "shalt thou not" / (LF), (1851) "will you not"
82. (LF), (1851) "you"
83. (LF), (1851) "do"
84. (LF), (1851) "lies"
85. (LF), (1851) "desires"
86. (LF), (1851) "you"
87. (LF), (1851) "you"
88. (LF), (1851) "shall"
89. (LF), (1851) "you"
90. (LF), (1851) "you"
91. (1851) omits "and thou shalt [verse 23] . . . gloried in his wickedness [verse 31]"

called perdition, for thou wast also before the world, [25] and it shall be
said, in time[92] to come, that these abominations were[93] had from Cain;
for he rejected the greater Counsel which was had from God. and this
is a cursing which I will put upon thee, except thou repent. [26] and
        Cain was
wroth, and listened not any more to the voice of the Lord, neither to
        Abel
his Brother, who walked in Holiness before the Lord, [27] and Adam
        also[94] and his
wife mourned before the Lord, because of cain and his brethren. [28]
        and it came
to pass that cain took one of his brother's[95] daughters to wife, and they
        loved
Satan more than God. [29] and Satan saith[96] unto cain, swear unto me
        by
thy throat; and if thou tell it thou shalt die; and swear thy brethren by
their heads, and by the living God, that they tell it not, for, if they tell
it, they shall surely die; and this that thy father
may not know it; and this day I will deliver thy brother Abel,
into thine hands, [30] and Satan sware[97] unto cain, that he would do

OT2 Page 12 (Moses 5:30–45)

according to his commands, and all these things were done in secret.
[31] and cain saith[98], truly I am Mahan[99], the Master of this great secret

---

92. OT1 "times"

93. OT1 "was"

94. 1902 omits "also", followed by 1921, 1981

95. OT1, OT2 "brothers" / CM "brother's", followed by *IV*, 1878, 1888 / 1902 "broth-
    ers'", followed by 1921, 1981

96. CM "said", followed by *IV*, 1878, 1888, 1902, 1921, 1981

97. OT1 "swore" / *IV* "swear", followed by 1878, 1888 / 1902 "sware", followed by
    1921, 1981

98. 1902 "said", followed by 1921, 1981

99. OT1 "Mahon"

that I may murder and get gain; Wherefore Cain was called master
Mahan[100]. and he gloried in his wickedness. [32] and cain went into
    the field
and cain[101] talked with \[102] Abel, his brother[103], and it came to pass
    that[104] while
they were in the field, ~~that~~[105] Cain rose up against \[106] Abel, his
    brother[107],
and Slew him. [33] and cain gloried in that which[108] he had done, say-
    ing, I
am free; surely the flocks of my brother falleth[109] into my
hands. [34] And[110] the Lord said unto cain, where is Abel, thy[111]
    brother. and
he said I know not, am I my brother's keeper? [35] and he[112] said, what
    hast[113] thou[114]
done? the voice of thy[115] brother's blood cries unto me from the
ground, [36] and now thou[116] shalt[117] be cursed from the Earth, which

---

100. OT1 "Mahon"
101. (LF), (1851) omit "cain"
102. (LF), (1851) insert "his brother"
103. (LF), (1851) omit "his brother"
104. (LF), (1851) omit "it came to pass that"
105. **Scribe undetermined** : CM, *IV*, 1878, 1888, 1902, 1921, 1981
106. (LF), (1851) insert "his brother"
107. (LF), (1851) omit "his brother"
108. "that which" : (LF), (1851) "what"
109. (LF), (1851) "will now fall"
110. (LF), (1851) "But"
111. (LF), (1851) "your"
112. (LF), (1851), CM "the Lord", followed by *IV*, 1878, 1888, 1902, 1921, 1981
113. (LF), (1851) "have"
114. (LF), (1851) "you"
115. (LF), (1851) "your"
116. (LF), (1851) "you"
117. (LF), (1851) "shall"

hath[118] opened her mouth, to receive thy[119] brother's blood, from thy[120] hand. [37] when thou[121] tillest[122] the ground, it[123] shall not henceforth yield unto thee[124] her strength; a fugitive, and a vagabond, \\[125] shalt[126] thou[127]

be in the Earth. [38] and cain said unto the Lord, Satan tempted me, because of my brother's flocks[128]; and I was \\[129] wroth[130] also[131], for his offering thou didst accept[132], and not[133] mine. \\[134] my punishment is greater than I can bear! [39] Behold, thou[135] hast[136] driven me out this day from the face of the ~~Earth~~ <Lord>[137] and from thy[138] face shall I be hid, \\[139]

and I shall be a fugitive, and a vagabond, in the Earth; and it shall

---

118. (LF), (1851) "has"

119. (LF), (1851) "your"

120. (LF), (1851) "your"

121. (LF), (1851) "you"

122. (LF), (1851) "till"

123. (LF), (1851) "she"

124. (LF), (1851) "you"

125. (LF), (1851) insert "also"

126. 1888 "shall" / 1902 "shalt", followed by 1921, 1981

127. "shalt thou" : (LF), (1851) "you shall"

128. OT1 "flock"

129. (LF), (1851) insert "also"

130. (LF), (1851) "angry"

131. (LF), (1851) omit "also"

132. 1888 "except" / 1902 "accept", followed by 1921, 1981 / "thou didst accept" : (LF), (1851) "was accepted"

133. (LF), (1851) omit "not"

134. (LF), (1851) insert "was not"

135. (LF), (1851) "you"

136. (LF), (1851) "have"

137. **SR** : CM, *IV*, 1878, 1888, 1902, 1921, 1981 / "the ~~Earth~~ <Lord>" : (LF), (1851) "men"

138. (LF), (1851) "your"

139. (LF), (1851) insert "also"

come to pass, ~~and~~[140] ~~every one~~ <that he>[141] that findeth[142] me will[143] slay
    me, because

of mine[144] ~~oath~~ <iniquities,>[145] for these things are not hid from the
    Lord. [40] and <I>[146] the

Lord Said unto him ~~Therefore~~[147] whosoever[148] slayeth[149] ~~cain~~ <thee>[150]
    vengeance

shall be taken on him seven fold[151]. and <I>[152] the Lord set a mark
    upon Cain lest

any finding him should kill him. [41] \[153] and Cain ~~went~~ <was shut>[154]
    out from the

presence of the Lord and \[155] his wife and many of his brethren and[156]
dwelt in the land of Nod, on the east of Eden [42] and Cain
knew his wife, and she conceived and bare Enoch and he also begat
many Sons and daughters and he builded a City and he called the
name of the City after the name of his Son Enoch. [43] and unto
Enoch was born Irad and other Sons and daughters and Irad begat

---

140. "and" not in OT1
141. **SR** : CM, *IV*, 1878, 1888, 1902, 1921, 1981
142. (LF), (1851) "finds"
143. OT1 "shall"
144. (LF), (1851) "my"
145. **SR** : CM, *IV*, 1878, 1888, 1902, 1921, 1981
146. **SR** : CM, *IV*, 1878, 1888, 1902, 1921, 1981
147. **SR** : CM, *IV*, 1878, 1888, 1902, 1921, 1981
148. (LF), (1851) "whoever"
149. (LF), (1851) "slays"
150. **SR** : CM, *IV*, 1878, 1888, 1902, 1921, 1981
151. "seven fold" : *IV* "seven-fold" / (1851), 1878 "sevenfold", followed by 1888, 1902,
    1921, 1981
152. **SR** : CM, *IV*, 1878, 1888, 1902, 1921, 1981
153. (1851) omits verses 41–59
154. **FGW** : CM, *IV*, 1878, 1888, 1902, 1921, 1981
155. CM inserts "with", followed by *IV*, 1878, 1888, 1902, 1921, 1981
156. CM omits "and", followed by *IV*, 1878, 1888, 1902, 1921, 1981

Mahujael and other Sons and daughters and Mahujael begat Mathusael, and other Sons and daughters. and Mathusael begat Lamech[157]
     [44] and
Lamech took unto himself two wives, the name of one
being Adah and the name of the other Zillah. [45] And Adah
bare Jabal; he was the father of such as dwell in tents, and
they were keepers of Cattle; and his Brother's name <was>[158] Jubal who
was the father of all such as handle the Harp and Organ.

OT2 Page 13 (Moses 5:46–58)

[46] And Zillah, she also bare Tubal Cain[159]; an instructor
of every artificer in Brass, and Iron, and the Sister of Tubal Cain[160]
was called Naamah. [47] and Lamech said unto his wives, Adah and
     Zillah
hear my voice, ye wives of Lamech; hearken unto my speech
for I have slain a man to my wounding, and a young man
to my hurt. [48] If Cain shall be avenged seven fold[161], truly
Lamech shall be seventy and seven fold. [49] For, Lamech having
entered into a covenant with Satan, after the manner of Cain
wherein he became Master Mahan[162], Master of that great secret
which was administered unto Cain, by Satan, and Irad[163], the Son
of Enoch, having known their secret began to reveal it unto
the sons of Adam; [50] wherefore, Lamech being angry, slew him
not like unto Cain, his brother Abel, for the sake of getting

---

157. OT1 "Lameh"
158. **FGW** corrects to OT1 : CM, *IV*, 1878, 1888, 1902, 1921, 1981
159. "Tubal Cain" : CM "Tubal-Cain"
160. "Tubal Cain" : CM "Tubal-Cain"
161. "seven fold" : *IV* "seven-fold" / 1878 "seven fold", followed by 1888, 1902 / 1921
      "sevenfold", followed by 1981
162. OT1 "Mahon"
163. OT1 "Irah"

gain, but he slew him for the oath's sake; [51] for, from the
days of Cain, there was a Secret combination and their works
were in the dark, and they knew every man his brother.
[52] Wherefore the Lord cursed Lamech[164] and his house and all they[165]
     that
had covenanted with Satan for they kept not the commandments of God And it displeased God and he ministered not unto them
and their works were abominations and began to spread among all
the Sons of men \[166] And it was among the Sons of men, [53] And
     among
the daughters of men these things were not spoken, Because
that Lamech had spoken the Secret unto his wives and they
Rebelled against him and declared these things abroad and had not
compassion.
[54] Wherefore[167] Lamech was despised, and cast out and came not
     among the
Sons of men lest he should die [55] and thus the works of darkness
began to prevail among all the Sons of men [56] and God cursed the
Earth with a sore curse and was angry with the wicked with
all the sons of men whom he had made [57] For they would not
hearken unto his voice nor believe on his only begotten Son
even him ~~which~~ <who>[168] he declared should come in the meridian of
time ~~which~~ <who>[169] was prepared from before the foundation of the
World. [58] And thus the Gospel began to be Preached from the beginni-
ng being declared by Holy Angels sent forth from the presen-
ce of God and by his own voice, and by the gift of the Holy Ghost.

---

164. OT1 "Lameck"

165. 1902 "them", followed by 1921, 1981

166. 1902, 1921 beginning of verse 53

167. CM "Where fore" / *IV* "Wherefore", followed by 1878, 1888, 1902, 1921, 1981

168. **SR** / CM "whom", followed by *IV*, 1878, 1888, 1902, 1921, 1981

169. **SR** : CM, *IV*, 1878, 1888, 1902, 1921, 1981

OT2 Page 14 (Moses 5:59–6:15)

[59] And thus all things were confirmed <unto Adam by an holy ordi-
nance>[170] and the Gospel Preached
and a decree sent[171] forth that it should be in the World until the
end thereof and thus it was amen.

---

170.   **SR** : CM, *IV*, 1878, 1888, 1902, 1921, 1981
171.   1888 "set" / 1902 "sent", followed by 1921, 1981

MOSES 6

[1] \\[1] And Adam hearkened unto the voice of God, and called upon
his Sons[2] to repent. [2] And Adam knew his wife again, and she
bare a Son, and he called his name Seth. And Adam glorified
the name of God, for he said, God hath appointed me another[3]
seed in stead[4] of Abel whom Cain slew. [3] And God revealed
himself unto Seth, and he rebelled not, But offered an acceptable
sacrifice like unto his brother Abel. and to him also was born
a Son, and he called his name Enos. [4] And then began these
men to call upon the name of the Lord; And the Lord blessed
them; [5] And a Book of remembrance was kept, in the which
was recorded in the language of Adam. For it was given unto
as many as called upon God, to write ~~with~~ <by>[5] the ~~finger~~ <spirit>[6] of
    insp-
iration; [6] And by them their children were taught to read
and write, Having a language which was pure and undefiled.

---

1. (1851) omits verses 1–42
2. 1888 "son" / 1902 "sons", followed by 1921, 1981
3. OT1 "an other", followed by CM / *IV* "another", followed by 1878, 1888, 1902,
   1921, 1981
4. "in stead" : OT1 "instead", followed by CM, *IV*, 1878, 1888, 1902, 1921, 1981
5. **SR** : CM, *IV*, 1878, 1888, 1902, 1921, 1981
6. **SR** : CM "Spirit", followed by *IV* / 1878 "spirit", followed by 1888, 1902, 1921,
   1981

[7] Now this <same priesthood which>⁷ was in the beginning ~~which~~⁸ shall
    be in the end
of the world <also>⁹. [8] Now this prophecy Adam spake, as he was
moved upon by the Holy Ghost¹⁰. And a genealogy was kept
of the Children of God And this was the Book of the generation¹¹
of Adam, Saying, In the day that God created man (in the likeness
of God created¹² he him)¹³ [9] in the image of his own body. Male
and female created he them and blessed them and called their names¹⁴
Adam, in the day when they were created, and became living
souls, in the land, upon the footstool of God. [10] And Adam lived
one Hundred and thirty¹⁵ years, and begat a son, in his own likeness
after his own¹⁶ image, and called his name seth.¹⁷ [11] and the days of
Adam after he had begotten Seth, were Eight hundred¹⁸ years. and he
begat many Sons and daughters. [12] and all the days that Adam lived

---

7. **SR** : CM, *IV*, 1878, 1888, 1902, 1921, 1981

8. **SR** : CM, *IV*, 1878, 1888, 1902, 1921, 1981

9. **SR** : CM, *IV*, 1878, 1888, 1902, 1921, 1981

10. "by the Holy Ghost" : not in OT1

11. OT1 "generations", followed by CM, *IV*, 1878, 1888, 1902, 1921, 1981

12. OT1 "made", followed by CM, *IV*, 1878, 1888, 1902, 1921, 1981

13. Parentheses not in OT1 / 1902 omits parentheses, followed by 1921, 1981

14. OT1 "name", followed by CM, *IV*, 1878, 1888, 1902, 1921, 1981

15. "one hundred and thirty" : OT1 "an 130"

16. Deleted in OT1

17. OT1 "Seth"

18. "Eight hundred" : OT1 "~~eight hundred~~ <eight hundred seventy>" : **OC** / On OT1
    (pages 11, 12, and 19) a number of changes were made to the ages of the Patriarchs
    after OT2 had been transcribed. Those changes are in Oliver Cowdery's handwriting.
    They were probably dictated by the Prophet no earlier than the summer of 1831 and
    before July 1832, when work resumed on the Genesis translation and OT2 had be-
    come the working manuscript. It appears that there was some uncertainty for a time
    regarding which of the two manuscripts would receive further correction.

were Nine hundred and thirty[19] years; and he[20] died. [13] Seth lived one
hundred and five[21] years, and begat Enos; and prophesied in all his
days, and taught (his son)[22] Enos in the ways of God. Wherefore
Enos prophesied also. [14] and Seth lived, after he begat Enos, eight
hundred and seven[23] years and begat many sons and daughters. [15] And the

OT2 Page 15 (Moses 6:15–28)

Children of men were numerous upon all the face of the
land, And in these[24] days, Satan had great dominion among
men, and raged in their hearts. And from thence forth[25] came wars
and blood shed.[26] And a man's hand was against his own brother
in administering death, because of secret works seeking for
power, [16] and[27] all the days of seth were nine hundred and twelve[28] years
and he died. [17] <and Enos lived ninety years and begat Cainan>[29] and
     Enos and the residue of the people of God, came out
from the land which was called shulon[30], and dwelt in a land of

---

19. "Nine hundred and thirty" : OT1 "~~nine hundred thirty~~ <one thousand>" : OC
20. 1888 omits "he" / 1902 inserts "he", followed by 1921, 1981
21. "one hundred and five" : OT1 "an 105"
22. "(his son)" : not in OT1 / CM omits parentheses, followed by *IV*, 1878, 1888, 1902, 1921, 1981
23. "eight hundred and seven" : OT1 "~~eight hundred seven~~ <eight hundred seventy-six>" : OC
24. CM "those", followed by *IV*, 1878, 1888, 1902, 1921, 1981
25. "thence forth" : *IV* "thenceforth", followed by 1878 / 1888 "henceforth" / 1902 "thenceforth", followed by 1921, 1981
26. "blood shed" : OT1 "blood sheds" / CM "bloodshed", followed by *IV*, 1878, 1888, 1902, 1921, 1981
27. 1888 deletes "and", followed by 1902, 1921, 1981
28. "nine hundred and twelve" : OT1 "~~nine hundred twelve~~ <nine hundred eighty-one>" : OC
29. SR : CM, *IV*, 1878, 1888, 1902, 1921, 1981
30. OT1 "Shulon"

Old Testament Manuscript 1, page 11, detail, showing revised ages of the Patriarchs; handwriting of John Whitmer and Emma Smith (last three lines), corrections by Oliver Cowdery; Moses 6:11–19

Promise, which he called after his own Son, whom he had named
~~Canaan~~ <Cainan.>[31] \[32] [18] And Enos lived, after he \[33] begat ~~Canaan~~
<Cainan,>[34] eight hundred
and fifteen[35] years, and begat many Sons and daughters. and all the day[36] of
Enos were nine hundred and five[37] years; and he died. [19] and ~~thus it
was~~[38]
\[39] ~~Canaan~~ <Cainan>[40] lived seventy[41] years, and begat Mahalaleel, and
~~Canaan~~ <Cainan>[42] live[43]
after he begat Mahalaleel, eight hundred and forty years[44]; and begat Sons
and daughters. And all the days of ~~Canaan~~ <Cainan>[45] were nine hundred
and ten[46] <years>[47]
and he died. [20] And Mahalaleel lived, sixty-five years[48], and begat
Jared, and Mahalaleel lived after he begat Jared eight hundred and thirty

---

31. **SR** corrects to OT1 : CM, *IV*, 1878, 1888, 1902, 1921, 1981
32. OT1 "<whom he begat when he was ninety years old>" : **OC**
33. 1888 inserts "had" / 1902 omits "had", followed by 1921, 1981
34. **SR** corrects to OT1 : CM, *IV*, 1878, 1888, 1902, 1921, 1981
35. "eight hundred and fifteen" : OT1 "~~eight hundred fifteen~~ <eight hundred fifty>" :
    OC
36. OT1 "days", followed by CM, *IV*, 1878, 1888, 1902, 1921, 1981
37. "nine hundred and five" : OT1 "~~nine hundred five~~ <nine hundred forty>" : **OC**
38. **SR** : CM, *IV*, 1878, 1888, 1902, 1921, 1981 / OT1 "thus it was amen"
39. OT1 "And"
40. **SR** : CM, *IV*, 1878, 1888, 1902, 1921, 1981 / OT1 "Cainan"
41. OT1 "~~seventy~~ <one hundred seventeen>" : **OC**
42. **SR** corrects to OT1 : CM, *IV*, 1878, 1888, 1902, 1921, 1981
43. OT1 "lived", followed by CM, *IV*, 1878, 1888, 1902, 1921, 1981
44. Not in OT1
45. **SR** corrects to OT1 : CM, *IV*, 1878, 1888, 1902, 1921, 1981
46. "nine hundred and ten" : OT1 "~~nine hundred and ten~~ <nine hundred fifty-seven>" :
    OC
47. **SR** corrects to OT1 : CM, *IV*, 1878, 1888, 1902, 1921, 1981
48. "sixty-five years" : OT1 "~~sixty and five years~~ <one hundred fifteen>" : **OC**

years, and begat sons and daughters. and all the days of Mahalaleel were
eight hundred and ninety-five[49] years[50]; and he died. [21] And Jared lived
    one[51]
hundred <and>[52] Sixty-two[53] years, and begat Enoch. and Jared lived after he
begat Enoch eight hundred years and begat sons and daughters. and Jared
taught Enoch in all the ways of God. [22] and this is the genealogy of
the sons of ~~God~~ <Adam>[54] ~~Which~~ <Who>[55] was the son[56] of[57] ~~Adam~~
    <God>[58] with whom God
himself conversed. [23] And they were preachers of righteousness and
spake, and prophesied, and called upon all men every where[59] to repent
And faith was taught unto the children of men. [24] And it came to
pass that all the days of Jared, were nine hundred sixty and two[60] years.
and he died. [25] and Enoch lived Sixty and five[61] years[62], and begat
    Methuselah [26] and it
came to pass, that Enoch Journeyed in the land, among the people;
and as he Journeyed, the spirit of God descended out of Heaven, and
    abode
upon him; [27] And he heard a voice from Heaven, saying, Enoch my

---

49. "eight hundred and ninety-five" : OT1 "~~eight hundred ninety-five~~ <nine hundred forty-five>" : **OC**
50. Not in OT1
51. OT1 "a"
52. **SR** corrects to OT1 : CM, *IV*, 1878, 1888, 1902, 1921, 1981
53. OT1 "sixty and two" / CM "sixty two", followed by *IV*, 1878, 1888, 1902, 1921, 1981
54. **SR** : CM, *IV*, 1878, 1888, 1902, 1921, 1981
55. **SR** : CM, *IV*, 1878, 1888, 1902, 1921, 1981
56. OT1 "sons"
57. CM "of of"
58. **SR** : CM, *IV*, 1878, 1888, 1902, 1921, 1981
59. "every where" : *IV* "everywhere", followed by 1878, 1888, 1902, 1921, 1981
60. "sixty and two" : CM "and sixty two", followed by *IV*, 1878, 1888, 1902, 1921, 1981
61. "sixty and five" : CM "sixty five", followed by *IV*, 1878, 1888, 1902, 1921, 1981
62. OT1 "year"

Son, prophesy unto this people, and say unto them, repent, for thus
saith the Lord, I am angry with this people, and my fierce anger
is kindled against them; For their hearts have waxed hard, and
their ears are dull of hearing, and their eyes cannot see afar[63] off;
[28] And for these many generations, even[64] since the day that I
created them, have they gone astray[65], and have denied me, and have
sought their own counsels in the dark, And in their own
abominations have they devised murder, and have not kept

OT2 Page 16 (Moses 6:28–40)

the commandments[66] which I gave unto their father, Adam.
[29] Wherefore, they have foresworn themselves, and by their oaths, they
have ~~eat unto~~ <brought upon>[67] themselves death. And an[68] Hell I have
    prepared
for them, if they repent not; [30] and this is a decree, which I have
sent forth in the beginning of the World, from mine[69] own
mouth, from the foundation thereof; and by the mouths of
my Servants, thy Fathers, have I decreed it; even as it shall be
sent forth into[70] the world, unto the end[71] thereof. [31] And when
Enoch had heard these words, he bowed himself to the Earth,
before the Lord; And spake before the Lord, Saying; why is
it that I have found favor in thy Sight, And am but a
lad, and all the people hate me, for I am slow of speech:
Wherefore am I thy Servant [32] And the Lord said unto Enoch,
go forth, and do as I have commanded thee, and no man shall

---

63. OT1 "a far"
64. (1879), 1902 "ever", followed by 1921, 1981
65. OT1 "a stray"
66. OT1 "commandment"
67. **SR** : CM, *IV*, 1878, 1888, 1902, 1921, 1981
68. 1902 "a", followed by 1921, 1981
69. 1902 "my", followed by 1921, 1981
70. OT1 "in", followed by CM, *IV*, 1878, 1888, 1902, 1921, 1981
71. 1902 "ends", followed by 1921, 1981

pierce thee. Open thy mouth, and it shall be filled, and[72] I will
give thee utterance; for all flesh is in my hands, and I will do
as seemeth me good. [33] Say unto this people, choose ye this
day ᴀ <to serve the Lord>[73] God who made you. [34] Behold, my spirit is
      upon you.
Wherefore, all thy words will I Justify. And the Mountains
shall flee before you, and the Rivers shall turn from their
course; and thou shalt abide in me, and I in you; Therefore
walk with me. [35] And the Lord spake unto Enoch, and said unto
him, anoint thine eyes with Clay, and wash them, and thou shalt
see; and he did so. [36] And he beheld the[74] spirits that God had
created, and he beheld also things which were not visible to
the natural eye[75], and from thenceforth[76], came the saying abroad
in the land, a seer hath the Lord raised up unto his
people. [37] And it came to pass, that Enoch went forth in the
land, among the people, standing upon the hills, and the high
places, and cried with a loud voice, testifying against their work[77],
and all men were offended Because of him, [38] and they came forth
to hear him, upon the high places, saying unto the Tent
keepers[78], tarry thou[79] <ye>[80] here, and keep the Tents, while we go yonder
to Behold the Seer, for he prophesieth; and there is a strange
thing in the land; a wild man hath come among us. [39] and it came
to pass, when they heard him, no man laid their[81] hands on him,
for fear came on all them that heard him, for he

---

72. Not in OT1

73. **SR** : CM, *IV*, 1878, 1888, 1902, 1921, 1981

74. 1888 omits "the" / 1902 inserts "the", followed by 1921, 1981

75. "to the natural eye" : not in OT1

76. CM "thence forth" / *IV* "thenceforth", followed by 1878, 1888, 1902, 1921, 1981

77. OT1 "works", followed by CM, *IV*, 1878, 1888, 1902, 1921, 1981

78. "tent keepers" : *IV* "tent-keepers" / 1878 "tent keepers", followed by 1888, 1902 /
     1921 "tent-keepers", followed by 1981

79. CM omits "thou", followed by *IV*, 1878, 1888, 1902, 1921, 1981

80. **Scribe undetermined**, post-1866 : CM, *IV*, 1878, 1888, 1902, 1921, 1981

81. CM omits "their", followed by *IV*, 1878, 1888, 1902, 1921, 1981

walked with God. [40] and there came a man unto him whose
name was Mahijah, and said unto him, tell us plainly

OT2 Page 17 (Moses 6:40–53)

Who thou art, and from whence thou came[82]? [41] and he saith[83] unto
them, I came out from the Land of Canaan[84], the land of my
fathers, a land of righteousness unto this day; and my father
taught me in all the ways of God. [42] And it came to pass,
as I Journeyed from the land of Canaan[85], by the Sea East, I
beheld a vision; and lo, the Heavens, I saw. And the Lord
spake with me, and gave me commandment; Wherefore, for
this cause, to keep the commandment, I ~~spake~~ <speak>[86] forth these
words. [43] and Enoch continued his speech, saying, The Lord which
spake with me, the same is the God of Heaven, and he is
my God, and your God, and ye are my Brethren; And why counsel ye yourselves[87], and deny the God of Heaven. [44] The Heavens
~~that~~[88] he made; the Earth is his footstool, and the foundation there-
of is his. Behold, he \[89] laid it, and hosts[90] of men hath he broug-
ht in upon the face thereof. [45] and death hath come upon our
Fathers; nevertheless, we know them, and cannot[91] deny, And even
the first of all we know, even Adam; [46] for a Book of
remembrance we have written among us, according to the

---

82. CM "comest", followed by *IV*, 1878, 1888, 1902, 1921, 1981

83. CM "said", followed by *IV*, 1878, 1888, 1902, 1921, 1981

84. OT1 "Cainan", followed by CM, *IV*, 1878, 1888, 1902, 1921, 1981

85. OT1 "Cainan", followed by CM, *IV*, 1878, 1888, 1902, 1921, 1981

86. **SR** corrects to OT1 : CM, *IV*, 1878, 1888, 1902, 1921, 1981

87. OT1 "your selves"

88. OT1 "hath", followed by (*EMS*), (1851) / probably **SR** : CM, *IV*, 1878, 1888, 1902, 1921, 1981

89. (*EMS*), (1851) "hath"

90. "and hosts" : OT1 "and host" / (*EMS*), (1851), 1878 "an host", followed by 1888, 1902, 1921, 1981

91. CM "can not" / *IV* "cannot", followed by 1878, 1888, 1902, 1921, 1981

pattern given by the finger of God; and it is given in our
own language. [47] And as Enoch spake forth the words of God,
the people trembled, and could not stand in[92] his presence.
[48] And he ~~saith~~ <said>[93] unto them, because that Adam fell we are,
and by his fall came death, and we are made partakers of misery and woe. [49] Behold, satan hath come among the Children of
men, And tempteth them to worship him And men
have become carnal, sensual and Devilish, and are shut out
from the presence of God. [50] but God hath made known unto our[94]
Fathers, that all men must repent. [51] And he called upon our
father Adam, by his own voice; Saying, I am God; I made
the world, and men before they were <in the flesh.>[95] [52] and he also
    said unto him
If thou wilt turn unto me, and hearken unto my voice and
believe, and repent of all thy[96] transgressions, and be baptized, even
~~by~~ <in>[97] water, in the name of mine only begotten Son, ~~which~~ <who>[98]
is full of grace and truth; ~~which~~ <who>[99] is Jesus Christ; the only
name which shall be given under Heaven, whereby salv-
ation shall come unto the children of men, and[100] ye shall
<receive the gift of the holy Ghost>[101] ask<ing>[102] all things in his name,
    and whatsoever[103] ye shall ask

---

92. OT1 "before", followed by (*EMS*), (1851)

93. **SR** : (1851), CM, *IV*, 1878, 1888, 1902, 1921, 1981

94. OT1 "my", followed by (*EMS*), (1851)

95. **SR** : CM, *IV*, 1878, 1888, 1902, 1921, 1981

96. OT1 "their"

97. **SR** : CM, *IV*, 1878, 1888, 1902, 1921, 1981

98. **SR** : CM, *IV*, 1878, 1888, 1902, 1921, 1981

99. **SR** : not in (*EMS*), (1851), CM, *IV*, 1878, 1888, 1902, 1921, 1981

100. (1851), 1878 omit "and", followed by 1888, 1902, 1921, 1981

101. **SR** : CM, *IV*, 1878, 1888, 1902, 1921, 1981

102. **SR** : CM, *IV*, 1878, 1888, 1902, 1921, 1981

103. (*EMS*), (1851) "whatever"

it shall be given <you>[104]. [53] And our father Adam spake[105] unto the
Lord and said why is it that men must repent and be baptized

OT2 Page 18 (Moses 6:53–63)

by <in>[106] water And the Lord said unto Adam Behold I have
forgiven thee thy transgression[107] in the garden of Eden [54] Hence[108]
came the saying abroad among the people that ~~Christ~~ <the son of God>[109]
    hath
atoned for original guilt. Wherein the sins of the parents
cannot be answered upon the heads of the Children, for they
are whole from the foundation of the world. [55] And the
Lord spake[110] unto Adam, Saying, inasmuch[111] as thy children
are conceived in sin, even so, when they begin to grow
up Sin conceiveth in their hearts, and they taste the bitter,
that they may know to prize the good. [56] and it is given
unto them to know good from evil; Wherefore, they are agents
unto <unto>[112] themselves. And I have given unto you another[113] law
and commandment; [57] Wherefore, teach it unto your Children,
that all men every where[114], must repent, or they can in
no wise[115] inherit the kingdom of God. For no unclean thing

---

104. **SR** : CM, *IV*, 1878, 1888, 1902, 1921, 1981

105. (*EMS*) "spoke"

106. **SR** : CM, *IV*, 1878, 1888, 1902, 1921, 1981

107. OT1 "transgressions", followed by (*EMS*), (1851), CM / *IV* "transgression", followed by 1878, 1888, 1902, 1921, 1981

108. (*EMS*), (1851) "Thence"

109. **SR** : CM, *IV*, 1878, 1888, 1902, 1921, 1981

110. (*EMS*) "spoke"

111. OT1 "in as much"

112. **SR** : not in (*EMS*), (1851), CM, *IV*, 1878, 1888, 1902, 1921, 1981

113. CM "an other" / (*EMS*), *IV* "another", followed by 1878, 1888, 1902, 1921, 1981

114. (1851), *IV* "everywhere", followed by 1878, 1888, 1902, 1921, 1981

115. "no wise" : 1921 "nowise", followed by 1981

Correction on a small piece of paper pinned to Old Testament Manuscript 2, page 18; handwriting of Sidney Rigdon; Moses 6:58–59

can dwell there or dwell in his presence; for, in the
language of Adam, Man of Holiness is his name; \[116] and the
name of his only begotten, is the son[117] ~~of~~ <a>[118] man ~~even Jesus
Christ~~[119] a righteous Judge ~~which~~ <who>[120] shall come <in the meridian of
time>[121]. [58] <~~Therefore~~>[122] ~~I give unto
you a commandment to teach these things freely unto
your Children Saying that in as much~~[123] ~~as they were born
into the World by <reason of>~~[124] ~~the fall which bringeth death by
water and blood and the Spirit which I have made and so became~~[125]
~~of dust a living soul even so ye must be born again
of water and the spirit and cleansed by blood even the blood
of mine only begotten into the mysteries of the kingdo-
m of Heaven~~ <Therefore, I give unto you a commandment, to teach
these things freely unto your children, saying,
[59] that by reason of transgression cometh the fall,
which fall bringeth death, And in as much[126] as they[127]
were born into the world by water, and blood, and
the spirit which I have made, and so became of

---

116. Joseph Smith's revision of the following sentence reads (modern punctuation pro-
posed): "And the name of his Only Begotten is the Son—a man, a righteous judge
who shall come in the meridian of time." Perhaps the intent was "... the Son of Man,
a righteous judge ... / (EMS), (1851), CM "... the Son of Man, even Jesus Christ,
a righteous judge ...", followed by IV, 1878, 1888, 1902, 1921, 1981

117. OT1 "Son"

118. SR : not in (EMS), (1851), CM, IV, 1878, 1888, 1902, 1921, 1981

119. SR : deletion not in (EMS), (1851), CM, IV, 1878, 1888, 1902, 1921, 1981

120. SR : CM, IV, 1878, 1888, 1902, 1921, 1981

121. SR : CM, IV, 1878, 1888, 1902, 1921, 1981

122. SR

123. "in as much" : (EMS), (1851) "inasmuch"

124. SR

125. (EMS), (1851) "become"

126. "in as much" : CM "inasmuch", followed by IV, 1878, 1888, 1902, 1921, 1981

127. CM "ye", followed by IV, 1878, 1888, 1902, 1921, 1981

dust a living soul; even so ye must be born
again, into the kingdom of heaven, of water, and of
the Spirit, and be cleansed by blood, even the
blood of mine only begotten.>[128]
that ye may[129] be sanctified from all Sin; and
enjoy the words of eternal life in this world; and eternal life
in the world to come; even immortal glory. [60] for, by the
water ye keep[130] the commandment; by the spirit ye are
Justified and by the blood ye are Sanctified. [61] ~~that~~ <Therefore>[131] ~~in~~
    ~~you~~ <it>[132] is
given <to abide in you>[133] the record of Heaven, the comforter, the ~~peace-~~
    ~~able~~
~~things of immortal glory~~ <keys of the kingdom of heaven>[134] the truth of
    all things that
which quickeneth all things, which maketh alive all
things, that which knoweth all things, and hath all power,
according <to>[135] wisdom, mercy, truth, Justice, and Judgment. [62] and
    now,
Behold, I say unto you, this is the plan of salvation
unto all men, <through>[136] the blood of mine only begotten, which[137]
shall come in the meridian of time. [63] And, Behold, all

---

128. **SR** : CM, *IV*, 1878, 1888, 1902, 1921, 1981

129. *IV* "might," followed by 1878, 1888, 1902, 1921, 1981

130. (*EMS*), (1851) "know"

131. **SR** : CM, *IV*, 1878, 1888, 1902, 1921, 1981

132. **SR** : CM, *IV*, 1878, 1888, 1902, 1921, 1981

133. **SR** : CM, *IV*, 1878, 1888, 1902, 1921, 1981

134. **SR** : not in (*EMS*), (1851), CM, *IV*, 1878, 1888, 1902, 1921, 1981

135. **SR** corrects to OT1 : (*EMS*), (1851), CM, *IV*, 1878, 1888, 1902, 1921, 1981

136. **SR** : CM, *IV*, 1878, 1888, 1902, 1921, 1981

137. CM "who", followed by *IV*, 1878, 1888, 1902, 1921, 1981

OT2 Page 19 (Moses 6:63–7:5)

Things have[138] their[139] likeness;
and all thing[140] are created and made to bear record[141] of me; both
things which are temporal, and things which are spiritual; things
which are in the Heavens above, and things which are on the
Earth, and things which are in the Earth and things which
are under the Earth; both above and beneath all things bear
Record of me. [64] And it came to pass, when the Lord had spoken
with Adam, our father, that Adam cried unto the
Lord, and he was caught away by the Spirit of the Lord, and was
carried down into the water, and was laid under the water, and was
brought forth out of the water; [65] and thus he was baptized, and
the spirit of God descended upon him, and thus he was born
of the spirit, and \[142] became quickened in the inner man. [66] and he
heard a voice out of heaven, saying, thou art baptized with fire
and with the Holy Ghost; this is the Record of the Father and the Son,
from hence forth[143] and forever[144]; [67] and thou art after the order of him
who was without beginning of days or end of years, from all
eternity to all eternity[145]. [68] Behold, thou art one in me, a Son
of God; and thus may all become my Sons: Amen.

---

138. OT1 "has", followed by (*EMS*)
139. OT1 "its", followed by (*EMS*)
140. OT1 "things", followed by (*EMS*), (1851), CM, *IV*, 1878, 1888, 1902, 1921, 1981
141. (1851) omits "record"
142. (*EMS*), (1851) "he"
143. "hence forth" : OT1 "henceforth", followed by (*EMS*), (1851), CM, *IV*, 1878, 1888, 1902, 1921, 1981
144. (1851), *IV* "for ever", followed by 1878, 1888, 1902 / 1921 "forever", followed by 1981
145. (1851) omits "to all eternity"

MOSES 7

[1] And it came to pass, that Enoch continued his speech, saying,
behold, our Father Adam taught these things, and many
have believed. And became[1] the sons of God; and many have believed not, and have[2] perished in their Sins, and are looking forth with
fear in torment, for the fiery indignation of the wrath of God,
to be poured out upon them. [2] And, from that time forth Enoch
began to prophesy, saying unto the people, that, as I was Jour-
neying And stood in[3] the place Mahujah[4], and[5] I[6] cried unto the Lord, \[7]
there came a voice out of \[8] Heaven, Saying, turn ye and get ye
upon the mount Simeon. [3] And it came to pass, that I turned
and went upon[9] the mount; And, as I stood upon the mount, I
beheld the Heavens open, and I was clothed upon with glory, [4] and
I saw the Lord; and[10] he stood before my face, and he talked with

---

1. OT1 "become", followed by (*EMS*), (1851) / *IV* "become", followed by 1878, 1888, 1902, 1921, 1981
2. (1851) omits "have"
3. (*EMS*), (1851), 1902 "upon", followed by 1921, 1981
4. (1851) "Manhujah"
5. (1851) omits "and"
6. **Scribe undetermined** : CM, *IV*, 1878, 1888, 1902, 1921, 1981
7. (1851) inserts "and"
8. (1851) inserts "the"
9. CM "up on", followed by *IV*, 1878, 1888, 1902, 1921, 1981
10. Not in OT1, (*EMS*), (1851)

me, even as a man talketh[11] one with another[12], face to face; and
he saith[13] unto me, look, and I will show unto thee[14] the world for
the space of many generations. [5] And it came to pass, that
I beheld in[15] the valley of[16] Shum, and Lo! a great people which

OT2 Page 20 (Moses 7:5–15)

Dwelt in tents, which were the people of Shum. [6] and again
the Lord said unto me, look, and I looked towards the North
and I beheld the people of Canaan[17], which dwelt in tents. [7] And
the Lord said unto me, prophesy; and I prophesied, Saying,
behold the people of Canaan[18], which are numerous, shall
go forth in battle array against the people of Shum, and
shall slay them, that they shall be utterly[19] destroyed. and
the people of Canaan[20] shall divide themselves in the land
and the land shall be barren and unfruitful, and none other
people shall dwell there but the people of Canaan[21].
[8] for, behold, the Lord shall curse the land with much
heat and the barrenness thereof shall go forth forever[22]. and there

---

11. (1851) "talks"

12. (*EMS*) "an other"

13. (1851), CM "said", followed by *IV*, 1878, 1888, 1902, 1921, 1981

14. (1851) "you"

15. (1851) omits "in"

16. (1851) omits "of"

17. CM "Cainan", followed by *IV*, 1878, 1888 / (*EMS*), (1851), 1902 "Canaan", followed by 1921, 1981

18. *IV* "Cainan", followed by 1878, 1888 / (*EMS*), (1851), 1902 "Canaan", followed by 1921, 1981

19. "be utterly" : OT1 "utterly be", followed by (*EMS*) / CM "be utterly", followed by *IV*, 1878, 1888 / 1902 "utterly be", followed by 1921, 1981

20. *IV* "Cainan", followed by 1878, 1888 / (*EMS*), (1851), 1902 "Canaan", followed by 1921, 1981

21. *IV* "Cainan", followed by 1878, 1888 / (*EMS*), (1851), 1902 "Canaan", followed by 1921, 1981

22. *IV* "for ever" / 1878 "forever", followed by 1888, 1902, 1921, 1981

was a[23] blackness come[24] upon all the children of canaan[25]
~~so~~[26] that[27] they were despised among all people. [9] And it
came to pass, that[28] the Lord said unto me look, and I, looked
and I[29] Beheld the land of Sharon, and the land of Enoch, and the
land of Omner, and the land of Heni, and the land of Shem,
and the land of Haner, and the land of Hananiah[30], and all the
inhabitants thereof. [10] and the Lord said unto me, go forth[31] to
this people, and say unto them, repent, lest I ~~shall~~[32] come
out and smite them with a curse, and they die. [11] And
he gave unto me a commandment, that I should baptize
in the name of the father, and of[33] the son[34], which[35] <who>[36] is full
of grace and truth, and \\[37] the Holy Ghost[38], which beareth[39] record
of the father and the Son. [12] And it came to pass, that Enoch
continued to call upon all the people, save it were the people

---

23. (1851) omits "a"

24. (1851), CM "came", followed by *IV*, 1878, 1888, 1902, 1921, 1981

25. *IV* "Cainan", followed by 1878, 1888 / (*EMS*), (1851), 1902 "Canaan", followed by 1921, 1981

26. **Scribe undetermined** corrects to OT1 : (*EMS*), (1851), CM, *IV*, 1878, 1888, 1902, 1921, 1981

27. 1902 "and" / 1921 "that", followed by 1981

28. Not in OT1

29. Not in (*EMS*), (1851)

30. OT1 "Hanannihah", followed by (*EMS*), (1851), CM , *IV*, 1878, 1888, 1902, 1921, 1981

31. (*EMS*), (1851), 1902 omit "forth", followed by 1921, 1981

32. **Scribe undetermined** : (1851), CM, *IV*, 1878, 1888, 1902, 1921, 1981

33. Not in (*EMS*), (1851)

34. OT1 "Son"

35. *IV* omits "which", followed by 1878, 1888 / (*EMS*), (1851), 1902 "which", followed by 1921, 1981

36. **Scribe undetermined**, post-1866, not in CM / *IV* "who", followed by 1878, 1888

37. 1902 inserts "of", followed by 1921, 1981

38. (1851) "Spirit"

39. (1851) "bears"

of Canaan[40], to repent [13] and so great was the faith of Enoch that he
led the people of God And their enemies came to battle
against them, and he spake the word of the Lord, and the Earth
trembled, and the Mountains fled, even according to his comm-
and and the Rivers (of water)[41] were turned out of their course and
the roar of the Lions[42] were[43] heard out of the wilderness, and all
Nations feared greatly, so powerful was the word of Enoch, and so great
was the power of the[44] language which god[45] had given him.
[14] There also came up a land out of the depth[46] of the Sea; and so
great was the fear of the enemies of the people of God, that
they fled and stood afar off[47], and went upon the land which came
up out of the depth[48] of the Sea. [15] And the Giants of the land,
also, stood afar off; and there went forth a curse upon all the[49]

OT2 Page 21 (Moses 7:15–29)

People which[50] fought against God, [16] and from that time forth, there
~~was~~ <were>[51] wars and bloodshed[52] among them; But the Lord came and
    dwelt with

---

40. *IV* "Cainan", followed by 1878, 1888 / (*EMS*), (1851), 1902 "Canaan", followed by
    1921, 1981
41. Parentheses not in OT1, (*EMS*), (1851) / CM omits parentheses, followed by *IV*,
    1878, 1888, 1902, 1921, 1981
42. (1851) "lion"
43. OT1 "was", followed by (*EMS*), (1851), CM, *IV*, 1878, 1888, 1902, 1921, 1981
44. (1851) omits "the"
45. OT1 "God"
46. OT1 "depths", followed by CM, *IV*, 1878, 1888 / (*EMS*), (1851), 1902 "depth", fol-
    lowed by 1921, 1981
47. 1888 "of"
48. OT1 "depths", followed by (*EMS*), (1851), CM, *IV*, 1878, 1888 / 1902 "depth", fol-
    lowed by 1921, 1981
49. 1902 omits "the", followed by 1921, 1981
50. 1902 "that", followed by 1921, 1981
51. **Scribe undetermined** : (1851), CM, *IV*, 1878, 1888, 1902, 1921, 1981
52. OT1 "bloodsheds", followed by (*EMS*), (1851)

his people, And they dwelt in righteousness. [17] and[53] the fear of the
    Lord was
upon all Nations, so great was the glory <of>[54] the Lord which was upon
his people. and the Lord blessed the land, and they were blessed upon
the mountains, and upon the high places, and did flourish. [18] and the
Lord called his people Zion[55]; because they were of one heart, and of[56]
one mind, and dwelt in righteousness. and there were[57] no poor among
them. [19] and Enoch continued his preaching in righteousness unto
the people of God. And it came to pass, in his days, that he built
a City that was called the City of Holiness, even Zion[58]. [20] And it
came to pass, that Enoch talked with the Lord, and he said unto the
Lord, Surely, Zion shall dwell in safety forever[59]. ~~But~~ <and>[60] the Lord
said unto Enoch, Zion have[61] I blessed, but the residue of the
people have I cursed. [21] And it came to pass, that the Lord
showed unto Enoch all the inhabitants of the Earth, and he beheld, and Lo! Zion, in process of time was taken up into Heaven
And the Lord said unto Enoch, behold mine[62] abode forever[63]. [22] and
Enoch, also beheld the residue of the people which were the sons
of Adam, And they were a mixture of all the seed of Adam, save
it were[64] the seed of Cain; for, the seed of Cain were black, and had

---

53. Not in OT1, (EMS), (1851) / 1902 omits "and", followed by 1921, 1981

54. **SR** corrects to OT1 : (EMS), (1851), CM, IV, 1878, 1888, 1902, 1921, 1981

55. 1902 "Zion", followed by 1921, 1981

56. (1851), CM omit "of", followed by IV, 1878, 1888, 1902, 1921, 1981

57. OT1 "was", followed by (EMS), (1851) / IV "was", followed by 1878, 1888, 1902, 1921, 1981

58. (EMS) "ZION" / (1851), 1878 "Zion", followed by 1888, 1902, 1921, 1981

59. IV "for ever" / 1878 "forever", followed by 1888, 1902, 1921, 1981

60. **SR** : not in (EMS), (1851), CM, IV, 1878, 1888, 1902, 1921, 1981

61. OT1 "hath", followed by (EMS)

62. (1851) "my"

63. (1851), IV "for ever", followed by 1878 / 1888 "forever", followed by 1902, 1921, 1981

64. 1981 "was"

Old Testament Manuscript 2, page 21, detail; handwriting of John Whitmer, corrections by Sidney Rigdon; Moses 7:24–29

not place among them. [23] and after that Zion was taken up into
Heaven, Enoch beheld, and lo! all the Nations of the Earth were
before him, [24] And there came generation upon generation, and
Enoch was high and lifted up, even in the bosom of the father,
(And \\[65] the son[66] of man;)[67] And, behold, the powers[68] of Satan were[69]
upon all the face of the Earth; [25] And he saw Angels descending
out of Heaven and he heard a loud voice, saying, woe! woe! be unto
the inhabitants of the Earth. [26] And he beheld Satan and he had a
great Chain in his hand, And ~~it~~ <he>[70] veiled the whole face of the
Earth with darkness, and he looked up and laughed, and his Angels
rejoiced. [27] and Enoch beheld Angels descending out of Heaven,
bearing testimony of the father, and of the[71] Son. and the Holy Ghost[72]
fell on many, and they were caught up by the power[73] of Heaven
into Zion. [28] And it came to pass, that ~~the God of Heaven~~ <Enoch>[74]
    look-
ed upon the residue of the people and \\[75] wept. And ~~Enoch bore~~
~~record of it Saying how is it~~ \\[76] ~~the heavens weep~~ <he beheld and lo! the
    heavens wept also>[77] and shed forth

---

65.   1902 inserts "of", followed by 1921, 1981

66.   OT1 "Son"

67.   Parentheses not in OT1, (*EMS*), (1851) / 1878 omits parentheses, followed by 1888,
      1902, 1921, 1981

68.   (*EMS*), (1851), 1902 "power", followed by 1921, 1981

69.   OT1 "was", followed by (*EMS*), (1851) / 1902 "was", followed by 1921, 1981

70.   **SR** : not in (*EMS*), (1851), CM, *IV*, 1878, 1888, 1902, 1921, 1981

71.   "of the" not in OT1, (*EMS*), (1851) / 1902 omits "of the", followed by 1921, 1981

72.   (1851) "Spirit"

73.   OT1 "powers", followed by (*EMS*), (1851) / 1902 "powers", followed by 1921, 1981

74.   **SR** : not in (*EMS*), (1851), CM, *IV*, 1878, 1888, 1902, 1921, 1981

75.   OT1 "he", followed by (*EMS*), (1851) / 1902 inserts "he", followed by 1921, 1981

76.   CM inserts "that", followed by *IV*, 1878, 1888, 1902, 1921, 1981

77.   **SR** : not in (*EMS*), (1851), CM, *IV*, 1878, 1888, 1902, 1921, 1981

~~her~~ <their>[78] tears as the rain upon the Mountains [29] And Enoch Said
unto the heavens[79] how is it that thou[80] canst[81] weep Seeing

OT2 Page 22 (Moses 7:29–41)

Thou[82] art[83] holy and from all eternity to all eternity, [30] and were
it possible that man could number the particles of \[84] Earth yea[85]
and[86] millions of such[87] Earths like this it would not be a begi-
nning to the number of thy[88] creations and thy[89] curtains are
stretched out still And ~~yet~~[90] thou[91] art[92] there and thy[93] ~~bosom~~ <presence>[94]
    is
there And also thou[95] art[96] Just thou[97] art[98] merciful and kind

---

78. **SR** : (1851), CM, *IV*, 1878, 1888, 1902, 1921, 1981

79. (*EMS*), (1851), CM "Lord", followed by *IV*, 1878, 1888, 1902, 1921, 1981

80. (1851) "you"

81. (1851) "can"

82. (1851) "you"

83. (1851) "are"

84. OT1 "the", followed by (*EMS*), (1851), CM, *IV*, 1878, 1888, 1902, 1921, 1981

85. (1851) omits "yea"

86. 1902 omits "and", followed by 1921, 1981

87. Not in OT1, (*EMS*), (1851), CM, *IV*, 1878, 1888, 1902, 1921, 1981

88. (1851) "your"

89. (1851) "your"

90. **SR** : CM, *IV*, 1878, 1888 / (*EMS*), (1851), 1902 insert "yet", followed by 1921, 1981

91. (1851) "you"

92. (1851) "are"

93. (1851) "your"

94. **SR** : not in (*EMS*), (1851), CM, *IV*, 1878, 1888, 1902, 1921, 1981

95. (1851) "you"

96. (1851) "are"

97. (1851) "you"

98. (1851) "are"

Old Testament Manuscript 2, page 22, detail; handwriting of John Whitmer,
corrections by Sidney Rigdon; Moses 7:29–33

forever[99] [31] \\[100] thou[101] hast[102] taken Zion to thine[103] own bosom from all
 thy[104] creations

from All eternity to all eternity ~~and~~[105] naught but peace Justice and
truth is the habitation of thy[106] throne and mercy shall go
before thy[107] face and have no end, how is it that[108] thou[109] canst[110]
weep? [32] the Lord said unto Enoch, behold, these thy[111] Brethren,
they are the workmanship of mine[112] own hands, and I gave unto
them their ~~knowledge~~ <intelligence>[113] ~~in the day that~~[114] ~~I created them~~[115]
 and in the
Garden of Eden ~~gave I unto~~[116] man ~~his~~ <had>[117] agency; [33] and unto
 thy[118] breth-
ren have I said, and also gave[119] commandment, that they should

---

99. *IV* "for ever" / 1878 "forever", followed by 1888, 1902, 1921, 1981

100. 1902 inserts "And", followed by 1921, 1981

101. (1851) "you"

102. (1851) "have"

103. (1851) "your"

104. (1851) "your"

105. **SR** : deletion not in (*EMS*), (1851), CM, *IV*, 1878, 1888, 1902, 1921, 1981

106. (1851) "your"

107. (1851) "your"

108. 1902 omits "that", followed by 1921, 1981

109. (1851) "you"

110. (1851) "can"

111. (1851) "your"

112. (1851) "my"

113. **SR** : not in (*EMS*), (1851), CM, *IV*, 1878, 1888, 1902, 1921, 1981

114. "that" not in OT1, (*EMS*), (1851) / 1902 omits "that", followed by 1921, 1981

115. **SR** : deletion not in (*EMS*), (1851), CM, *IV*, 1878, 1888, 1902, 1921, 1981

116. **SR** : deletion not in (*EMS*), (1851), CM, *IV*, 1878, 1888, 1902, 1921, 1981

117. **SR** : not in (*EMS*), (1851), CM, *IV*, 1878, 1888, 1902, 1921, 1981

118. (1851) "your"

119. (1851), 1902 "given", followed by 1921, 1981

love one another, and that they should ~~Choose me their father~~ <serve me
   their God>[120]
but, Behold, they are without affection, and they hate their own
blood; [34] and the fire of mine[121] indignation is kindled against them,
   and
in my hot displeasure will I send in the floods upon them, for
my fierce anger is kindled against them. [35] Behold, I am God
and[122] man of holiness is my name, man of council[123] is my name,
and endless, and eternal is my name also. [36] Wherefore, I can stretch
   forth
mine[124] hands, and hold all the Creations which I have
made. And mine[125] eye can pierce them also. And among all the
workmanship of mine[126] hands[127], there has not been so great wickedness as among thy[128] brethren; [37] But, behold, their sins shall be
upon the heads of their fathers; Satan shall be their ~~father~~ <master>[129]
and misery shall be their doom; and the whole heavens shall
weep over them, even all the workmanship of mine[130] hands.
Wherefore should not the heavens weep, seeing these Shall suffer.
[38] But, behold, these which thine[131] eyes are upon shall perish in

---

120. **SR** : not in (*EMS*), (1851), CM, *IV*, 1878, 1888, 1902, 1921, 1981

121. (1851) "my"

122. Not in OT1, (*EMS*), (1851), CM, *IV*, 1878, 1888, 1902, 1921, 1981

123. (1851), 1878 "Counsel", followed by 1888, 1902, 1921, 1981

124. (1851), CM "my", followed by *IV*, 1878, 1888 / (*EMS*), 1902 "mine", followed by
      1921, 1981

125. (1851) "my"

126. (1851), CM "my", followed by *IV*, 1878, 1888 / (*EMS*), 1902 "mine", followed by
      1921, 1981

127. OT1 "hand", followed by (*EMS*), (1851)

128. (1851) "your"

129. **SR** : not in (*EMS*), (1851), CM, *IV*, 1878, 1888, 1902, 1921, 1981

130. (1851), CM "my", followed by *IV*, 1878, 1888 / (*EMS*), (1879), 1902 "mine", fol-
      lowed by 1921, 1981

131. (1851) "your"

the floods, and behold, I will shut them up; A prison have I
prepared for them [39] And ~~that~~ <he>[132] ~~which~~ <whom>[133] I have chosen
　　~~hath~~ <has>[134] pled[135]
before my face. Wherefore, he suffereth[136] for their sins, in
as much[137] as they will repent, in the day that my Chosen
~~will~~ <Shall>[138] return unto me; And until that day, they shall be in
torment. [40] Wherefore, for this shall the heavens[139] weep, yea, and
all the workmanship of mine[140] hands. [41] And it came to pass
that the Lord spake unto Enoch, and told Enoch all the

OT2 Page 23 (Moses 7:41–51)

Doings of the Children of men, Wherefore, Enoch knew, and
looked upon their wickedness, and their misery, and wept, and stretched
forth his arms, ~~and his heart swelled wide as~~ <and he beheld>[141] eternity,
　　and his
bowels yearned, and all eternity shook, [42] and Enoch \|[142] saw Noah
also[143] And his family, That the posterity of all the Sons of
Noah should be saved with a temporal salvation. [43] wherefore
~~he~~ <Enoch>[144] saw that Noah built an Ark and \|[145] the Lord smiled upon

---

132. **SR** : not in (*EMS*), (1851), CM, *IV*, 1878, 1888, 1902, 1921, 1981

133. **SR** : not in (*EMS*), (1851), CM, *IV*, 1878, 1888, 1902, 1921, 1981

134. **SR** : (1851), CM, *IV*, 1878, 1888 / (*EMS*), 1902 "hath", followed by 1921, 1981

135. (1851) "pleaded"

136. (1851) "suffers"

137. "in as much" : OT1 "inasmuch", followed by (*EMS*), (1851), CM, *IV*, 1878, 1888, 1902, 1921, 1981

138. **Scribe undetermined**, post-1866, corrects to OT1 : (*EMS*), (1851), CM, *IV*, 1878, 1888, 1902, 1921, 1981

139. OT1 "heaven"

140. (1851), CM "my", followed by *IV*, 1878, 1888 / (*EMS*), 1902 "mine", followed by 1921, 1981

141. **SR** : not in (*EMS*), (1851), CM, *IV*, 1878, 1888, 1902, 1921, 1981

142. 1902 inserts "also", followed by 1921, 1981

143. 1902 omits "also", followed by 1921, 1981

144. **SR** : CM, *IV*, 1878, 1888, 1902, 1921, 1981

145. 1902 inserts "that", followed by 1921, 1981

it and held it in his own[146] hand but upon the residue of the
wicked came[147] the floods \[148] and swallowed them up. [44] and as Enoch
saw thus[149], he had bitterness of Soul, and wept over his breth-
ren, and said unto the Heavens, I will refuse to be comforted
but, the Lord said unto Enoch, lift up your heart and be
glad, and look. [45] And it came to pass, that Enoch ~~beheld~~ <looked>[150].
     And
from Noah he beheld all the families of the Earth; and he
cried unto the Lord, saying, when shall the day of the Lord
come? When shall the blood of the righteous be shed that
all they that mourn may be sanctified, and have eternal
life? [46] And the Lord said, it shall be in the meridian of time
in the days of wickedness and vengeance [47] And, behold, Enoch saw
the day of the coming of the son of man, even in the flesh
And ~~he~~ <his>[151] ~~saw and~~ <soul>[152] rejoiced, saying, the righteous is lifted
          up, and
the Lamb is slain from the foundation of the world; and
through faith I am in the bosom of the father; And, behold,
Zion is with me.[153] [48] and it came to pass, that Enoch looked upon \[154]
Earth, and he heard a voice from the bowels thereof, saying, woe! woe!
is me the mother of men![155] I am pained, I am weary, because

---

146. (1851) omits "own"

147. 1902 omits "came", followed by 1921, 1981

148. 1902 inserts "came", followed by 1921, 1981

149. 1902 "this", followed by 1921, 1981

150. **Scribe undetermined**, post-1866, corrects to OT1 : (*EMS*), (1851), CM, *IV*, 1878, 1888, 1902, 1921, 1981

151. **Scribe undetermined** corrects to OT1 : (*EMS*), (1851), CM, *IV*, 1878, 1888, 1902, 1921, 1981

152. **Scribe undetermined** corrects to OT1 : (*EMS*), (1851), CM, *IV*, 1878, 1888, 1902, 1921, 1981

153. (*EMS*) "me?"

154. OT1 "the", followed by (*EMS*), (1851), CM, *IV*, 1878, 1888, 1902, 1921, 1981

155. (*EMS*) "men?"

of the wickedness of my Children,[156] when shall I rest, and be cleansed from the ~~wickedness~~ <filthiness>[157] which has[158] gone forth out of me?
when will my creator sanctify me, that I may rest, and righteousness for a season abide upon my face. [49] And when Enoch
heard the Earth mourn, he wept, and cried unto the Lord, saying
O Lord wilt[159] thou[160] not have compassion upon the Earth,
wilt[161] thou[162] not bless the children of Noah? [50] And it came to
pass, that Enoch continued his cry unto the Lord, Saying, I ask
thee[163] O Lord, in the name of thine[164] Only Begotten ~~even Jesus
Christ~~[165], That thou[166] wilt[167] have mercy upon Noah, and his seed,
that the Earth might[168] never more be covered by the floods[169]
[51] and the Lord could not with hold[170] and he covenanted with ~~Noah~~
          <Enoch>[171] and
~~swore~~ <sware>[172] unto him with[173] an oath, that he would stay the floods

---

156. (*EMS*) "children?"

157. **Scribe undetermined**, post-1866, corrects to OT1 : (*EMS*), (1851), CM, *IV*, 1878,
     1888, 1902, 1921, 1981

158. 1902 "is", followed by 1921, 1981

159. (1851) "will"

160. (1851) "you"

161. (1851) "will"

162. (1851) "you"

163. (1851) "you"

164. OT1 "thy", followed by (*EMS*) / (1851) "your"

165. **SR** : deletion not in (*EMS*), (1851), CM, *IV*, 1878, 1888, 1902, 1921, 1981

166. (1851) "you"

167. (1851) "will"

168. (1851) "may"

169. (*EMS*) "floods?"

170. "with hold" : OT1 "withhold", followed by (*EMS*), (1851), CM, *IV*, 1878, 1888,
     1902, 1921, 1981

171. **SR** : (1851), CM, *IV*, 1878, 1888, 1902, 1921, 1981

172. **SR** : CM, *IV*, 1878, 1888, 1902, 1921, 1981

173. 1888 omits "with" / 1902 inserts "with", followed by 1921, 1981

OT2 Page 24 (Moses 7:51–62)

That he would call upon the children of Noah [52] And he
sent forth an unalterable decree that <from>[174] a remnant of his seed
should ~~always be found among~~ <come>[175] all Nations while the Earth
should stand. [53] And the Lord said, blessed is ~~him~~ <he>[176] through
whose
seed the[177] Messiah ~~should~~ <shall>[178] come; For he saith[179], I am the[180]
Messiah,
the King of Zion; the rock of Heaven, which is broad as
eternity, and[181] whoso cometh[182] in at the gate and climbeth[183] up by
me, shall never fall. Wherefore, blessed are they of ~~which~~ <whom>[184]
I have spoken, for they shall come forth with songs of
everlasting Joy. [54] And it came to pass, that Enoch cried
unto the Lord, saying, when the Son of man cometh[185] in
the flesh shall the Earth rest? I pray thee[186] show me these
things. [55] And the Lord said unto Enoch, look, and he looked
and beheld the son[187] of man lifted upon[188] the cross, after the
manner of men. [56] And he heard a loud voice, and the Heavens
were veiled; and all the creation[189] of God mourned; And the

---

174. **SR** : not in (*EMS*), (1851), CM, *IV*, 1878, 1888, 1902, 1921, 1981
175. **SR** : not in (*EMS*), (1851), CM, *IV*, 1878, 1888, 1902, 1921, 1981
176. **SR** : (1851), CM, *IV*, 1878, 1888, 1902, 1921, 1981
177. Not in OT1, (*EMS*), (1851), CM, *IV*, 1878, 1888, 1902, 1921, 1981
178. **SR** : (1851), CM, *IV*, 1878, 1888, 1902, 1921, 1981
179. (1851) "says"
180. Not in OT1, (*EMS*), (1851), CM, *IV*, 1878, 1888, 1902, 1921, 1981
181. (*EMS*), (1851), 1902 omit "and", followed by 1921, 1981
182. (1851) "comes"
183. (1851) "climbs"
184. **SR** : (1851), CM, *IV*, 1878, 1888, 1902, 1921, 1981
185. (1851) "comes"
186. (1851) "you"
187. OT1 "Son"
188. CM "up on", followed by *IV*, 1878, 1888, 1902, 1921, 1981
189. CM "creations", followed by *IV*, 1878, 1888, 1902, 1921, 1981

Old Testament Manuscript 2, page 24, detail; handwriting of John Whitmer;
corrections by Sidney Rigdon; Moses 7:51–55

Earth groaned; and the rocks were rent; and the saints arose, and
were[190] crowned at the right hand of the Son of man with
crowns of glory. [57] and as many of the spirits as were in Prison
came forth and stood on the right hand of God. and the remainder
were[191] reserved in chains of darkness until the Judgment of
the great day. [58] And ~~again~~[192] Enoch wept, and cried unto the
Lord again[193], Saying, when Shall the Earth rest? [59] and Enoch
beheld the Son of man ascend up unto the Father; and he
called unto the Lord, Saying, wilt[194] thou[195] not come again
upon the Earth? for, in as much[196] as thou[197] art[198] God, and I know
thee[199] and thou[200] hast[201] sworn unto me and commanded me that I
should ask in the name of thine[202] only begotten. Thou[203] hast[204]
made me and given unto[205] me a right to thy[206] throne, and not of
myself but through thine[207] own grace; wherefore, I ask

---

190. OT1 "was"

191. OT1 "was", followed by (*EMS*)

192. **SR** : deletion not in (*EMS*), (1851), CM, *IV*, 1878, 1888, 1902, 1921, 1981

193. (1851), CM omit "again", followed by *IV*, 1878, 1888, 1902, 1921, 1981

194. (1851) "will"

195. (1851) "you"

196. "in as much" : OT1 "inasmuch", followed by (*EMS*), (1851) / CM "in as much" / *IV* "inasmuch", followed by 1878, 1888 / 1902 "forasmuch", followed by 1921, 1981

197. (1851) "you"

198. (1851) "are"

199. (1851) "you"

200. (1851) "you"

201. (1851) "have"

202. (1851) "your"

203. (1851) "you"

204. (1851) "have"

205. *IV* omits "unto", followed by 1878, 1888 / 1902 inserts "unto", followed by 1921, 1981

206. (1851) "your"

207. (1851) "your"

thee[208] if thou[209] wilt[210] not come again on the Earth? [60] and the Lord
said unto Enoch, As I live, even so will I come in the last
days, in the days[211] of wickedness and vengeance, to fulfill the
oath which I have[212] made unto you concerning the Children of
Noah. [61] And the day shall come that the Earth shall rest. But
before that day \[213] the Heavens shall[214] be darkened, and a veil of darkness
shall cover the Earth; and the Heavens shall shake and also the
Earth. A[215] great tribulation[216] shall be among the children of
men, but my People will I preserve; [62] and righteousness will I

OT2 Page 25 (Moses 7:62–8:4)

Send down out of Heaven, ~~and~~[217] truth will I send forth out
of[218] the Earth, to bear testimony of mine[219] Only Begotten; his resu-
rrection from the dead; yea, and also the resurrection of all men.
And righteousness and truth will I cause to sweep the Earth as \[220]

---

208. (1851) "you"
209. (1851) "you"
210. (1851) "will"
211. 1888 omits "in the days" / 1902 inserts "in the days", followed by 1921, 1981
212. *IV* omits "have", followed by 1878, 1888 / (*EMS*), (1851), 1902 insert "have", fol-
    lowed by 1921, 1981
213. (1851) inserts "shall"
214. (1851) omits "shall"
215. OT1 "And", followed by (*EMS*), (1851), CM, *IV*, 1878, 1888, 1902, 1921, 1981
216. OT1 "tribulations", followed by (*EMS*), (1851), CM, *IV*, 1878, 1888, 1902, 1921,
    1981
217. Probably **SR** : deletion not in (*EMS*), (1851), CM, *IV*, 1878, 1888, 1902, 1921,
    1981
218. Not in OT1, CM / (*EMS*), *IV* insert "of", followed by 1878, 1888, 1902, 1921,
    1981
219. (1851) "my"
220. OT1 "with", followed by (*EMS*), (1851)

~~the~~ <with a>[221] flood, to gather out mine[222] own[223] elect from the four
   quarters
of the Earth, unto a place which I shall prepare; an[224] holy
City, that my people may gird up their loins, and be looking
forth for the time of my coming; for there shall be my
tabernacle, and it shall be called Zion[225], a New Jerusalem.
[63] and the Lord said unto Enoch, then shalt[226] thou[227] and all thy[228] City
meet them there; and we will receive them into our bosom;
and they shall see us, And we will fall upon their necks, and
they shall fall upon our necks, and we will kiss each other
[64] and there shall be mine[229] abode, and it shall be Zion which shall
come forth out of all the creations which I have made; and for
the space of a thousand years shall[230] the Earth \[231] rest. [65] and it came
to pass, that Enoch saw the day[232] of the coming of the son of man,
in the last days, to dwell on the Earth, in righteousness, for
the space of a thousand years. [66] but before that day, he saw
great tribulations[233] among the wicked; and he also saw the Sea,

---

221. **Scribe undetermined**, probably post-1866 : CM, *IV*, 1878, 1888, 1902, 1921, 1981
   / (*EMS*), (1851) "a"
222. (1851) "my"
223. (1879), 1902 omit "own", followed by 1921, 1981
224. (1851) "a"
225. (*EMS*) "ZION" / (1851), 1878 "ZION", followed by 1888 / 1902 "Zion", followed
   by 1921, 1981
226. (1851) "shall"
227. (1851) "you"
228. (1851) "your"
229. (1851) "my"
230. 1902 omits "shall", followed by 1921, 1981
231. 1902 inserts "shall", followed by 1921, 1981
232. (*EMS*), (1851) "days"
233. OT1 "tribulation", followed by CM, *IV*, 1878, 1888 / (*EMS*), (1851), 1902 "tribu-
   lations", followed by 1921, 1981

that it was troubled, and men's hearts failing them looking forth
with fear for the Judgments[234] of the Almighty God, Which should
come upon the wicked. [67] And the Lord showed Enoch all things,
even unto the end of the world. And he saw the day of the
righteous, the hour of their redemption, and received a fullness of Joy.
[68] And all the days of Zion, in the days of Enoch, were three
hundred and sixty five years. [69] And Enoch and all his people
walked with God, And he dwelt in the midst of Zion.
And it came to pass, that Zion was not, for God received
it up into his own bosom; and from thence went forth the
saying, Zion is fled[235]

---

234. *IV* "judgment", followed by 1878, 1888 / (*EMS*), (1851), 1902 "judgments", followed by 1921, 1981

235. "Zion is fled" : (1851), 1878 "ZION IS FLED", followed by 1888 / 1902 "ZION IS FLED", followed by 1921, 1981

MOSES 8

[1] \¹ \² [2] and it came to pass, that Methuselah,
the son of Enoch, was not taken, that the covenants of the
Lord might be fulfilled which he made to Enoch; for he
truly covenanted with Enoch, that Noah should ~~come by~~ <be of>³ the fruit
of his loins. [3] And it came to pass, that Methuselah Prophesied, that from his loins should Spring all the kingdoms
of the Earth, (~~from~~ <through>⁴ Noah.) And he took glory unto himself;
[4] and there came forth a great famine into the land, And the
Lord cursed the Earth with a sore curse, And many of the

OT2 Page 26 (Moses 8:4–21)

inhabitants thereof died. [5] And it came to pass, that Methuselah
lived one hundred Eighty and seven years⁵ and begat Lamech; [6] and

---

1. (1851) omits verses 1–12
2. OT1 "<And all the days of Enoch were four hundred thirty years.>" : **OC**, followed
   by CM / *IV* ". . . four hundred and thirty years", followed by 1878, 1888, 1902,
   1921, 1981
3. **SR** : CM, *IV*, 1878, 1888, 1902, 1921, 1981
4. **SR** : CM, *IV*, 1878, 1888, 1902, 1921, 1981
5. "one hundred Eighty and seven years" : OT1 "~~an hundred eighty and seven years~~
   <two hundred eighteen years>" : **OC** / CM "one hundred and eighty seven years",
   followed by *IV*, 1878, 1888, 1902, 1921, 1981

137

Methuselah lived, after he begat Lamech, seven hundred \\[6]
eighty and[7] two years and begat sons and Daughters. [7] and all the days
of Methuselah were nine hundred and sixty and nine years[8]; and he
died. [8] and Lamech lived an[9] hundred \\[10] eighty and[11] two years And be-
gat
a son, [9] and he called his name Noah, saying, This son shall
comfort us concerning our work and toil of our hands, because
of the ground which the Lord hath cursed. [10] and Lamech lived
after he begat Noah, five hundred and[12] ninety and[13] five years, and
begat sons and daughters. [11] and all the days of Lamech were seven
hundred \\[14] seventy and[15] seven years; and he died. [12] ~~And <it came to
pass that when>~~[16] ~~Noah was five
hundred years old And Noah <he>~~[17] ~~begat Shem Ham and Japheth.~~ <And
Noah was four Hundred and fifty years old and begat
Japheth, and forty two years afterward[18], he begat shem
of her who was the Mother of Japheth, and
when he was five hundred years old, he begat Ham.>[19]

---

6. CM inserts "and", followed by *IV*, 1878, 1888, 1902, 1921, 1981

7. CM omits "and", followed by *IV*, 1878, 1888, 1902, 1921, 1981

8. "nine hundred and sixty and nine years" : OT1 "~~nine Hundred Sixty and nine years~~
   <one thousand>" : **OC** / CM "nine hundred and sixty nine years", followed by *IV*,
   1878, 1888, 1902, 1921, 1981

9. CM "one", followed by *IV*, 1878, 1888, 1902, 1921, 1981

10. CM inserts "and", followed by *IV*, 1878, 1888, 1902, 1921, 1981

11. CM omits "and", followed by *IV*, 1878, 1888, 1902, 1921, 1981

12. Not in OT1

13. CM omits "and", followed by *IV*, 1878, 1888, 1902, 1921, 1981

14. CM inserts "and", followed by *IV*, 1878, 1888, 1902, 1921, 1981

15. CM omits "and", followed by *IV*, 1878, 1888, 1902, 1921, 1981

16. **SR**

17. **SR**

18. CM "afterwards", followed by *IV*, 1878, 1888 / 1902 "afterward", followed by 1921,
    1981

19. **SR** : CM, *IV*, 1878, 1888, 1902, 1921, 1981

[13] And ~~it came to pass that~~[20] Noah and his Sons hearkened unto
the Lord and gave heed and they were called the sons of God [14] and
when these men began to multiply on the face of the earth
and daughters were born unto them that[21] the sons of men saw
that their[22] daughters were fair \[23] they took them wives even
as they chose. [15] and the Lord said unto Noah the daughters of thy
sons have sold themselves For Behold mine anger is kindled
against the sons of men for they will not hearken to my
voice. [16] And it[24] came to pass that Noah prophesied and taught
the things of God even as it was in the beginning [17] and the
Lord said unto Noah my spirit shall not always strive
with man for he shall know that all flesh shall die Yet his
days shall be an hundred and twenty years and if men do not
repent I will send in the[25] floods upon them. [18] And in those days
there were giants on the Earth And they sought Noah to take
away his life but the Lord was with Noah and the power of the Lord
was upon him [19] and the Lord ordained Noah after his own[26] order and
      com-
manded him that he should go forth and declare his Gospel unto
the children of men even as it was given unto Enoch. [20] And
it came to pass that Noah called upon the children of[27] men that they
should repent but they hearkened not unto his words [21] and also
after that they had heard him they came up before him Saying
Behold we are the Sons of God have we not taken unto ourse-
lves \[28] daughters of men and are we not eating and drinking

---

20. **SR** : CM, *IV*, 1878, 1888, 1902, 1921, 1981

21. CM omits "that", followed by *IV*, 1878, 1888, 1902, 1921, 1981

22. 1902 "those", followed by 1921, 1981

23. *IV* inserts "and", followed by 1878, 1888, 1902, 1921, 1981

24. OT1 "it it"

25. (1851) "my"

26. (1851) omits "own"

27. "the children of" not in OT1, (*EMS*), (1851)

28. OT1 "the", followed by (*EMS*), (1851), CM, *IV*, 1878, 1888, 1902, 1921, 1981

OT2 Page 27 (Moses 8:21–30)

and marrying and given[29] in marriage and[30] our wives bear unto us children and the same are mighty men which are like unto them[31] of
old men of great renown and they hearkened not unto[32] the words of
    Noah. [22] and
God saw that the wickedness of man[33] had become great in the Earth
And every man was lifted up in the imagination of the thoughts of his heart being only evil continually. [23] And it came to
pass that Noah continued his preaching unto the people
saying hearken and give heed unto my words [24] Believe and repent of
    your
sins and be baptized in the name of Jesus Christ the son[34] of God
even as our fathers did[35] and ye shall receive the \[36] Holy Ghost that
ye may have all things made manifest and if you[37] do not \[38] this
the floods will come in upon you. Nevertheless they heark-
ened not. [25] And it repented Noah and his heart was pained that
the Lord \[39] made man on the Earth and it grieved him at the[40]
heart [26] And the Lord said I will destroy man whom I have created

---

29. (1851), 1878 "giving", followed by 1888, 1902, 1921, 1981
30. Not in (*EMS*), (1851)
31. 1888 "men", followed by 1902, 1921, 1981
32. (*EMS*), (1851) "to"
33. (*EMS*), (1851), 1878 "men", followed by 1888, 1902, 1921, 1981
34. OT1 "Son"
35. 1902 omits "did", followed by 1921, 1981
36. OT1 "gift of the", followed by (*EMS*), (1851)
37. (1851), 1878 "ye", followed by 1888, 1902, 1921, 1981
38. OT1 "do", followed by (*EMS*)
39. OT1 "had", followed by (*EMS*), (1851) / 1902 inserts "had", followed by 1921, 1981
40. OT1 "his", followed by (*EMS*), (1851)

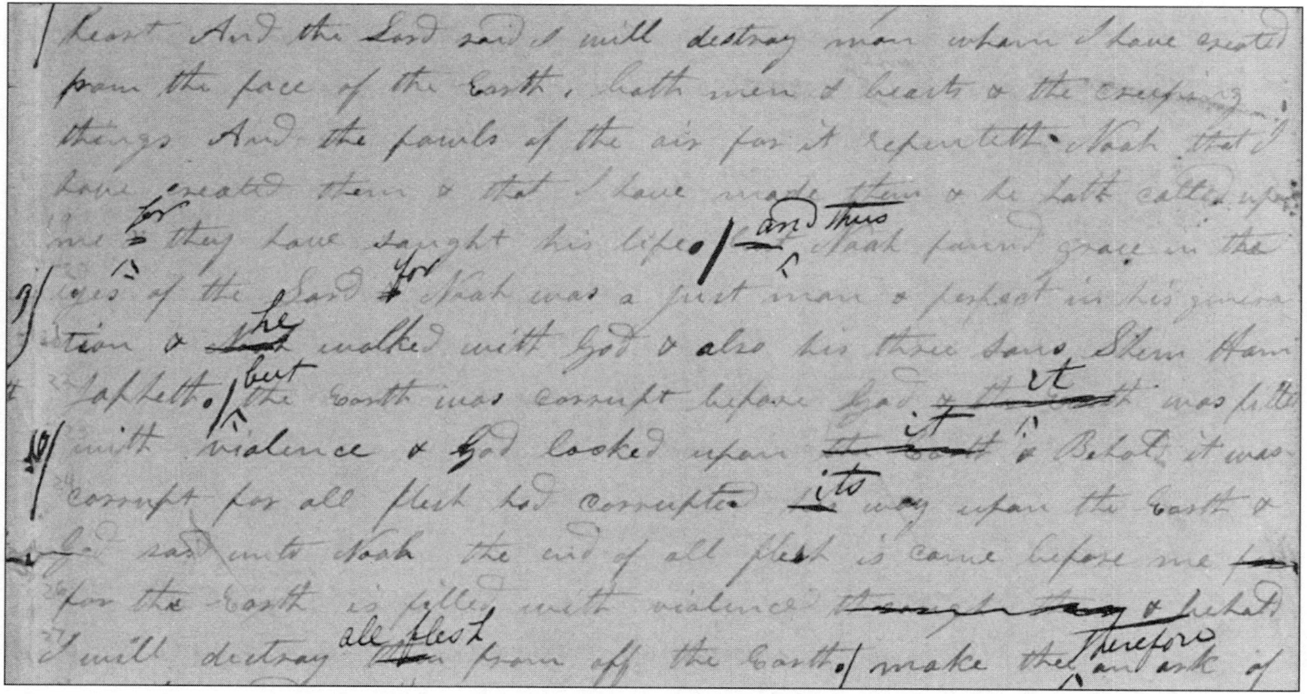
heart And the Lord said I will destroy man whom I have created
from the face of the Earth, both men & beasts & the creeping
things And the fowls of the air for it repenteth Noah that I
have created them & that I have made them & he hath called upon
me for they have sought his life. and thus Noah found grace in the
eyes of the Lord for Noah was a just man & perfect in his genera
tion & he walked with God & also his three sons Shem Ham
Japheth. but the Earth was corrupt before God & it was filled
with violence & God looked upon it & Behold it was
corrupt for all flesh had corrupted its way upon the Earth &
God said unto Noah the end of all flesh is come before me
for the Earth is filled with violence & behold
I will destroy all flesh from off the Earth. make thee therefore an ark of

Old Testament Manuscript 2, page 27, detail; handwriting of John Whitmer, corrections by Sidney Rigdon; Moses 8:25–30

from the face of the Earth, both men[41] and beasts[42] and the creeping
things And the fowls of the air for it repenteth Noah that I
have created them and that I have made them and he hath called upon
me ~~and~~ <for>[43] they have sought his life. [27] ~~but~~ <and thus>[44] Noah
      found grace in the
eyes of the Lord ~~and~~ <for>[45] Noah was a Just man and perfect in his generation[46] and ~~Noah~~ <he>[47] walked with God and[48] also his three sons Shem
      Ham \\[49]
Japheth. [28] <but>[50] the Earth was corrupt before God ~~and the Earth~~[51]
      <it>[52] was filled
with violence [29] and God looked upon ~~the Earth~~ <it>[53] and Behold it was
corrupt for all flesh had corrupted ~~his~~ <its>[54] way upon the Earth [30] and
God said unto Noah the end of all flesh is come before me
for the Earth is filled with violence ~~through them~~[55] and behold
I will destroy ~~them~~ <all flesh>[56] from off the Earth.

---

41. OT1 "man", followed by (*EMS*), (1851) / *IV* "man", followed by 1878, 1888, 1902,
     1921, 1981

42. OT1 "beast", followed by (*EMS*), (1851) / *IV* "beast," followed by 1878, 1888, 1902,
     1921, 1981

43. **SR** : CM, *IV*, 1878, 1888, 1902, 1921, 1981

44. **SR** : CM, *IV*, 1878, 1888, 1902, 1921, 1981

45. **SR** : CM, *IV*, 1878, 1888, 1902, 1921, 1981

46. OT1 "generations", followed by (*EMS*), (1851)

47. **SR** : CM, *IV*, 1878, 1888, 1902, 1921, 1981

48. 1902 "as did", followed by 1921, 1981

49. OT1 "and", followed by (*EMS*), (1851), CM, *IV*, 1878, 1888, 1902, 1921, 1981

50. **SR** : not in (*EMS*), (1851), CM, *IV*, 1878, 1888, 1902, 1921, 1981

51. Deletion not in (*EMS*), (1851)

52. **SR** : CM "and it", followed by *IV*, 1878, 1888, 1902, 1921, 1981

53. **SR** : not in (*EMS*), (1851), CM, *IV*, 1878, 1888, 1902, 1921, 1981

54. **SR** : CM, *IV*, 1878, 1888, 1902, 1921, 1981 / (1851) "their"

55. **SR** : CM, *IV*, 1878, 1888, 1902, 1921, 1981

56. **SR** : CM, *IV*, 1878, 1888, 1902, 1921, 1981

MANUSCRIPT TEXT

The following transcript of the Book of Moses is the text as Joseph Smith left it to the Church and as recorded on the original manuscripts. In transcribing this text, I have adhered to the following two guidelines:

1. The text is as Joseph Smith dictated it to his scribes. This includes (a) the Old Testament Manuscript 1 text and (b) later corrections he made to the text, recorded by him and his scribes on both Old Testament Manuscript 1 and Old Testament Manuscript 2.[1]

2. Grammar, spelling, capitalization, and punctuation have been standardized to current usage.[2]

In the preparation of the Manuscript Text, there has been no effort made to select a favored reading or to pick and choose among alternatives. There has been no consideration given to familiar or established readings, nor to doctrinal implications. This is simply the text that Joseph Smith prepared on the original manuscripts of his New Translation of the Bible, without

---

1. Transcription anomalies made by John Whitmer on Old Testament Manuscript 2 that were incorporated later into revisions by Joseph Smith are preserved in the Manuscript Text.

2. Almost all of the standardization was accomplished by John Whitmer and the compilers of the editions. For example, "These words *was* spoken" (Moses 1:42; OT1) is changed to "These words *were* spoken" (OT2). The use of archaic language, however,

the changes that were made in subsequent years by copyists, editors, and typesetters. The words are presented as the Prophet left them, but with grammar, spelling, capitalization, and punctuation standardized. Only in the area of punctuation was subjective judgment necessary on a few occasions. But even then, punctuation decisions infrequently have implications for how the text is understood. For convenience, the verse numbers of the current Book of Moses have been inserted, but no paragraphing has been added.

The Manuscript Text was not prepared to be an alternative to the text contained in the Pearl of Great Price. Its intent is simply to show the results of an examination into the history of the Selections from the Book of Moses. The text brings us as close as is now possible to the book's original revelation and to the Prophet who brought it forth. In doing so, it bears testimony both to the message and to Joseph Smith's calling to reveal it to the world.

---

has not been standardized in this text. Like the Book of Mormon, the Book of Moses shows fluidity in the use of archaic and modern personal pronouns (*thee, thou, ye, you*), possessive pronouns (*my, mine*), and associated verbal conjugations. Joseph Smith dictated both *thou/thee* and *you* for the second person singular (Moses 1:40–41; 2:1). In correcting a passage, he modernized "this earth upon which *thou standest*, and *thou shalt* write" to "this earth upon which *you stand*, and *you shall* write" (Moses 1:40), and "the book which *thou shalt* write, . . . like unto *thee*" to "the book which *you shall* write, . . . like unto *you*" (Moses 1:41). But these changes were not made consistently through the manuscripts. Alternative forms like "*my* hands" (Moses 6:32) and "*mine* hands" (Moses 7:36–37) exist both on the original manuscripts and in the current edition of the Pearl of Great Price. Joseph Smith also dictated both *hath* (Moses 6:49–50) and *has* (Moses 1:18; 7:36), and in one place he modernized *hath* to *has* when he made a later revision (Moses 7:39).

MOSES 1

¹The words of God, which he spake unto Moses at a time when Moses was caught up into an exceeding high mountain. ²And he saw God face to face, and he talked with him, and the glory of God was upon him; therefore, he could endure his presence. ³And God spake unto Moses, saying: "Behold, I am the Lord God Almighty, and endless is my name, for I am without beginning of days or end of years. And is this not endless? ⁴And behold, thou art my son. Wherefore, look, and I will show thee the workmanship of mine hands—but not all, for my works are without end, and also my words, for they never cease. ⁵Wherefore, no man can behold all my works except he behold all my glory. And no man can behold all my glory and afterwards remain in the flesh on the earth. ⁶And I have a work for thee, Moses, my son. And thou art in similitude of mine Only Begotten, and mine Only Begotten is and shall be the Savior, for he is full of grace and truth. But there is none other God beside me, and all things are present with me, for I know them all. ⁷And now behold, this one thing I show unto thee, Moses, my son, for thou art in the world, and now I show it thee." ⁸And it came to pass that Moses looked and beheld the world upon which he was created. And as Moses beheld the world and the ends thereof, and all the children of men which are and which were created, of the same he greatly marveled and wondered. ⁹And the presence of God withdrew from Moses that his glory was not upon him, and Moses was left unto himself. And as he was left unto himself, he fell unto the earth. ¹⁰And it came to pass that it was for the space of many hours before he did again receive his natural strength like unto man. And he said unto himself: "Now for this once I know that man is nothing, which thing I never had supposed. ¹¹But now mine eyes have beheld God—but not my natural eyes but my spiritual, for my natural eyes could not have beheld, for I should have withered and died in his presence. But his glory

was upon me and I beheld his face, for I was transfigured before him."
[12]And now it came to pass that when Moses had said these words, behold,
Satan came tempting him, saying: "Moses, son of man, worship me."
[13]But Moses lifted up his eyes and looked upon Satan and said: "Who art
thou? For behold, I am a son of God in the similitude of his Only
Begotten. And where is thy glory that I should worship thee? [14]For behold, I could not look upon God except his glory should come upon me.
And I was transfigured before him, but I can look upon thee in the natural man. [15]Surely, blessed be the name of my God, for his Spirit hath not
altogether withdrawn from me. I say 'Where is thy glory?' for it is blackness unto me, and I can judge between thee and God. For God said unto
me: 'Worship God, for him only shalt thou serve.' [16]Get thee hence,
Satan, deceive me not. For God said unto me: 'Thou art after the similitude of mine Only Begotten.' [17]And he also gave unto me commandment
when he called unto me out of the burning bush, saying: 'Call upon God
in the name of mine Only Begotten, and worship me.'" [18]And again
Moses said: "I will not cease to call upon God; I have other things to inquire of him. For his glory has been upon me, and it is glory unto me.
Wherefore, I can judge between him and thee. Depart hence, Satan."
[19]And now when Moses had said these words, Satan cried with a loud
voice and rent upon the earth and commanded, saying: "I am the Only
Begotten, worship me." [20]And it came to pass that Moses began to fear
exceedingly, and as he began to fear, he saw the bitterness of hell.
Nevertheless, calling upon God he received strength, and he commanded,
saying: "Depart hence, Satan, for this one God only will I worship, which
is the God of glory." [21]And now Satan began to tremble, and the earth
shook. And Moses received strength and called upon God in the name of
his Son, saying to Satan: "Depart hence." [22]And it came to pass that Satan
cried with a loud voice, with weeping and wailing and gnashing of teeth,
and departed hence, yea from the presence of Moses, that he beheld him
not. [23]And now of this thing Moses bore record, but because of wickedness it is not had among the children of men. [24]And it came to pass that
when Satan had departed from the presence of Moses, that Moses lifted
up his eyes unto heaven, being filled with the Holy Ghost, which beareth
record of the Father and the Son. [25]And calling upon the name of God, he
beheld again his glory, for it rested upon him. And he heard a voice say-

ing: "Blessed art thou, Moses, for I, the Almighty, have chosen thee. And thou shalt be made stronger than the many waters, for they shall obey thy command even as my commandments. [26]And lo I am with you, even to the end of thy days, for thou shalt deliver my people from bondage, even Israel my chosen." [27]And it came to pass, as the voice was still speaking, he cast his eyes and beheld the earth, yea even all the face of it. And there was not a particle of it which he did not behold, discerning it by the Spirit of God. [28]And he beheld also the inhabitants thereof, and there was not a soul which he beheld not. And he discerned them by the Spirit of God. And their numbers were great, even as numberless as the sand upon the sea shore. [29]And he beheld many lands, and each land was called earth, and there were inhabitants upon the face thereof. [30]And it came to pass that Moses called upon God, saying: "Show me, I pray thee, why these things are so, and by whom thou madest them." [31]And behold, the glory of God was upon Moses, that Moses stood in the presence of God, and he talked with him face to face. And the Lord God said unto Moses: "For mine own purpose have I made these things. Here is wisdom, and it re-maineth in me. [32]And by the word of my power have I created them, which is mine Only Begotten Son, full of grace and truth. [33]And worlds without number have I created, and I also created them for mine own purpose, and by the same I created them, which is mine Only Begotten. [34]And the first man of all men have I called Adam, which is many. [35]But only an account of this earth and the inhabitants thereof give I unto you. For behold, there are many worlds which have passed away by the word of my power, and there are many also which now stand, and numberless are they unto man. But all things are numbered unto me, for they are mine, and I know them." [36]And it came to pass that Moses spake unto the Lord, saying: "Be merciful unto thy servant, O God, and tell me concerning this earth and the inhabitants thereof, and also the heavens, and then thy servant will be content." [37]And the Lord God spake unto Moses of the heavens, saying: "These are many, and they cannot be numbered unto man. But they are numbered unto me, for they are mine. [38]And as one earth shall pass away and the heavens thereof, even so shall another come. And there is no end to my works, neither my words. [39]For behold, this is my work and my glory, to bring to pass the immortality and the eternal life of man. [40]And now Moses, my son, I will speak unto you concerning this earth upon which you stand, and you shall write the things which I shall speak. [41]And in a day when the children of men shall esteem my words as naught and take many of them from the book which you shall write, behold, I will raise up another like unto you, and they shall be had again among the children of men, among even as many as shall believe." [42]These words were spoken unto Moses in the mount, the name of which shall not be known among the children of men.

Moses 2

[1]And it came to pass that the Lord spake unto Moses, saying: "Behold, I reveal unto you concerning this heaven and this earth. Write the words which I speak. I am the Beginning and the End, the Almighty God. By mine Only Begotten I created these things. Yea, in the beginning I created the heaven and the earth upon which thou standest. [2]And the earth was without form and void. And I caused darkness to come up upon the face of the deep. And my Spirit moved upon the face of the waters, for I am God. [3]And I, God, said: 'Let there be light.' And there was light. [4]And I, God, saw the light, and the light was good. And I, God, divided the light from the darkness. [5]And I, God, called the light Day, and the darkness I called Night. And this I did by the word of my power, and it was done as I spake. And the evening and the morning were the first day. [6]And again I, God, said: 'Let there be a firmament in the midst of the waters.' And it was so, even as I spake. And I said: 'Let it divide the waters from the waters.' And it was done. [7]And I, God, made the firmament and divided the waters—yea, the great waters under the firmament from the waters which were above the firmament. And it was so, even as I spake. [8]And I, God, called the firmament Heaven. And the evening and the morning were the second day. [9]And I, God, said: 'Let the waters under the heaven be gathered together unto one place.' And it was so. And I, God, said: 'Let there be dry land.' And it was so. [10]And I, God, called the dry land Earth, and the gathering together of the waters called I the Seas. And I, God, saw that all things which I had made were good. [11]And I, God, said: 'Let the earth bring forth grass—the herb yielding seed, the fruit tree yielding fruit

after his kind, and the tree yielding fruit, whose seed should be in itself upon the earth.' And it was so, even as I spake. [12]And the earth brought forth grass—every herb yielding seed after his kind, and the tree yielding fruit, whose seed should be in itself after its kind. And I, God, saw that all things which I had made were good. [13]And the evening and the morning were the third day. [14]And I, God, said: 'Let there be lights in the firmament of the heaven to divide the day from the night. And let them be for signs and for seasons and for days and for years. [15]And let them be for lights in the firmament of the heaven to give light upon the earth.' And it was so. [16]And I, God, made two great lights—the greater light to rule the day and the lesser light to rule the night. And the greater light was the sun, and the lesser light was the moon. And the stars also were made, even according to my word. [17]And I, God, set them in the firmament of the heaven to give light upon the earth—[18]and the sun to rule over the day and the moon to rule over the night, and to divide the light from the darkness. And I, God, saw that all things which I made were good. [19]And the evening and the morning were the fourth day. [20]And I, God, said: 'Let the waters bring forth abundantly the moving creature that hath life, and fowl which may fly above the earth in the open firmament of heaven.' [21]And I, God, created great whales, and every living creature that moveth, which the waters brought forth abundantly after their kind, and every winged fowl after his kind. And I, God, saw that all things which I had created were good. [22]And I, God, blessed them, saying: 'Be fruitful, and multiply, and fill the waters in the sea. And let fowl multiply in the earth.' [23]And the evening and the morning were the fifth day. [24]And I, God, said: 'Let the earth bring forth the living creature after his kind—cattle, and creeping thing, and beast of the earth after their kind.' And it was so. [25]And I, God, made the beasts of the earth after their kind, and cattle after their kind, and everything which creepeth upon the earth after his kind. And I, God, saw that all these things were good. [26]And I, God, said unto mine Only Begotten, which was with me from the beginning: 'Let us make man in our image, after our likeness.' And it was so. And I, God, said: 'Let them have dominion over the fish of the sea, and over the fowl of the air, and over the cattle, and over all the earth, and over every creeping thing that creepeth upon the earth.' [27]So I, God, created man in mine own image. In the image of mine Only Begotten created I him, male and female created I them. [28]And I, God, blessed them. And I, God, said unto them: 'Be fruitful, and multiply, and replenish the earth, and subdue it. And have dominion over the fish of the sea, and over the fowl of the air, and over every living thing that moveth upon the earth.' [29]And I, God, said unto man: 'Behold, I have given you every herb bearing seed which is upon the face of all the earth, and every tree in the which shall be the fruit of a tree, yielding seed. To you it shall be for meat. [30]And to every beast of the earth, and to every fowl of the air, and to everything that creepeth upon the earth wherein I grant life, there shall be given every clean herb for meat.' And it was so, even as I spake. [31]And I, God, saw everything that I had made. And behold, all things which I had made were very good. And the evening and the morning were the sixth day."

MOSES 3

[1]"Thus the heaven and the earth were finished, and all the host of them. [2]And on the seventh day I, God, ended my work and all things which I had made. And I rested on the seventh day from all my work, and all things which I had made were finished. And I, God, saw that they were good. [3]And I, God, blessed the seventh day and sanctified it, because that in it I had rested from all my work which I, God, had created and made. [4]And now behold, I say unto you that these are the generations of the heaven and of the earth when they were created, in the day that I, the Lord God, made the heaven and the earth, [5]and every plant of the field before it was in the earth, and every herb of the field before it grew. For I, the Lord God, created all things of which I have spoken spiritually before they were naturally upon the face of the earth. For I, the Lord God, had not caused it to rain upon the face of the earth. And I, the Lord God, had created all the children of men and not yet a man to till the ground. For in heaven created I them. And there was not yet flesh upon the earth, neither in the water, neither in the air. [6]But I, the Lord God, spake, and there went up a mist from the earth and watered the whole face of the ground. [7]And I, the Lord God, formed man from the dust of the ground and breathed into his nostrils the breath of life. And man became a living soul,

the first flesh upon the earth, the first man also. Nevertheless, all things were before created, but spiritually were they created and made according to my word. [8]And I, the Lord God, planted a garden eastward in Eden. And there I put the man whom I had formed. [9]And out of the ground made I, the Lord God, to grow every tree naturally that is pleasant to the sight of man. And man could behold it. And it became also a living soul, for it was spiritual in the day that I created it, for it remaineth in the sphere in which I, God, created it—yea, even all things which I prepared for the use of man. And man saw that it was good for food. And I, the Lord God, planted the tree of life also in the midst of the garden, and also the tree of knowledge of good and evil. [10]And I, the Lord God, caused a river to go out of Eden to water the garden. And from thence it was parted and became into four heads. [11]And I, the Lord God, called the name of the first Pison, and it compasseth the whole land of Havilah, where I, the Lord, created much gold. [12]And the gold of that land was good, and there was bdellium and the onyx stone. [13]And the name of the second river was called Gihon, the same that compasseth the whole land of Ethiopia. [14]And the name of the third river was Hiddekel, that which goeth towards the east of Assyria. And the forth river was Euphrates. [15]And I, the Lord God, took the man and put him into the Garden of Eden to dress it and to keep it. [16]And I, the Lord God, commanded the man, saying: 'Of every tree of the garden thou mayest freely eat. [17]But of the tree of the knowledge of good and evil, thou shalt not eat of it. Nevertheless, thou mayest choose for thyself, for it is given unto thee. But remember that I forbid it, for in the day that thou eatest thereof, thou shalt surely die.' [18]And I, the Lord God, said unto mine Only Begotten that it was not good that the man should be alone. Wherefore, I will make a help meet for him. [19]And out of the ground I, the Lord God, formed every beast of the field and every fowl of the air and commanded that they should come unto Adam to see what he would call them. And they were also living souls. For I, God, breathed into them the breath of life and commanded that whatsoever Adam called every living creature, that should be the name thereof. [20]And Adam gave names to all cattle and to the fowl of the air and to every beast of the field. But as for Adam, there was not found a help meet for him. [21]And I, the Lord God, caused a deep sleep to fall upon Adam, and he slept. And I took one of his ribs and closed up the flesh in the stead thereof. ²²And the rib which I, the Lord God, had taken from man made I a woman and brought her unto the man. ²³And Adam said: 'This I know now is bone of my bones and flesh of my flesh. She shall be called woman, because she was taken out of man.' ²⁴Therefore shall a man leave his father and his mother and shall cleave unto his wife. And they shall be one flesh. ²⁵And they were both naked, the man and his wife, and were not ashamed."

MOSES 4

¹And I, the Lord God, spake unto Moses, saying: "That Satan, whom thou hast commanded in the name of mine Only Begotten, is the same which was from the beginning. And he came before me, saying: 'Behold, send me. I will be thy son, and I will redeem all mankind that one soul shall not be lost. And surely I will do it. Wherefore, give me thine honor.' ²But behold, my beloved Son, which was my beloved and chosen from the beginning, said unto me: 'Father, thy will be done, and the glory be thine forever.' ³Wherefore, because that Satan rebelled against me and sought to destroy the agency of man, which I, the Lord God, had given him—and also that I should give unto him mine own power—by the power of mine Only Begotten I caused that he should be cast down. ⁴And he became Satan, yea, even the devil, the father of all lies, to deceive and to blind men and to lead them captive at his will, even as many as would not hearken unto my voice. ⁵And now the serpent was more subtle than any beast of the field which I, the Lord God, had made. ⁶And Satan put it into the heart of the serpent—for he had drawn away many after him—and he sought also to beguile Eve, for he knew not the mind of God. Wherefore, he thought to destroy the world. ⁷And he said unto the woman: 'Yea, hath God said: "Ye shall not eat of every tree of the garden"?' And he spake by the mouth of the serpent. ⁸And the woman said unto the serpent: 'We may eat of the fruit of the trees of the garden. ⁹But of the fruit of the tree which thou beholdest in the midst of the garden, God hath said: "Ye shall not eat of it, neither shall ye touch it, lest ye die."' ¹⁰And the serpent said unto the woman: 'Ye shall not surely die.

¹¹For God doth know that in the day ye eat thereof, then your eyes shall be opened and ye shall be as gods, knowing good and evil.' ¹²And when the woman saw that the tree was good for food and that it became pleasant to the eyes, and a tree to be desired to make her wise, she took of the fruit thereof and did eat and gave also unto her husband with her, and he did eat. ¹³And the eyes of them both were opened. And they knew that they had been naked, and they sewed fig leaves together and made themselves aprons. ¹⁴And they heard the voice of the Lord God as they were walking in the garden in the cool of the day. And Adam and his wife went to hide themselves from the presence of the Lord God amongst the trees of the garden. ¹⁵And I, the Lord God, called unto Adam and said unto him: 'Where goest thou?' ¹⁶And he said: 'I heard thy voice in the garden, and I was afraid because I beheld that I was naked, and I hid myself.' ¹⁷And I, the Lord God, said unto Adam: 'Who told thee that thou wast naked? Hast thou eaten of the tree whereof I commanded thee that thou shouldst not eat, if so thou shouldst surely die?' ¹⁸And the man said: 'The woman whom thou gavest me and commandedst that she should remain with me, she gave me of the fruit of the tree, and I did eat.' ¹⁹And I, the Lord God, said unto the woman: 'What is this thing which thou hast done?' The woman said: 'The serpent beguiled me, and I did eat.' ²⁰And I, the Lord God, said unto the serpent: 'Because thou hast done this, thou shalt be cursed above all cattle and above every beast of the field. Upon thy belly shalt thou go, and dust shalt thou eat all the days of thy life. ²¹And I will put enmity between thee and the woman, between thy seed and her seed. He shall bruise thy head, and thou shalt bruise his heel.' ²²Unto the woman I said: 'I will greatly multiply thy sorrow and thy conception; in sorrow thou shalt bring forth children. And thy desire shall be to thy husband, and he shall rule over thee.' ²³And unto Adam I, the Lord God, said: 'Because thou hast hearkened unto the voice of thy wife and hast eaten of the fruit of the tree of which I commanded thee, saying: "Thou shalt not eat of it," cursed shall be the ground for thy sake. In sorrow shalt thou eat of it all the days of thy life. ²⁴Thorns also and thistles shall it bring forth to thee. And thou shalt eat the herb of the field. ²⁵By the sweat of thy face shalt thou eat bread until thou shalt return unto the ground, for thou shalt surely die. For out of it wast thou taken. For dust thou wast, and unto dust shalt thou return.' ²⁶And Adam called his wife's

name Eve, because she was the mother of all living. For thus have I, the Lord God, called the first of all women, which are many. [27]Unto Adam also and to his wife did I, the Lord God, make coats of skin and clothed them. [28]And I, the Lord God, said unto mine Only Begotten: 'Behold, the man is become as one of us to know good and evil. And now lest he put forth his hand and partake also of the tree of life and eat and live forever, [29]therefore I, the Lord God, will send him forth from the Garden of Eden to till the ground from whence he was taken. [30]For as I, the Lord God, live, even so my words cannot return void. For as they go forth out of my mouth, they must be fulfilled.' [31]So I drove out the man. And I placed at the east of the Garden of Eden cherubim and a flaming sword, which turned every way to keep the way of the tree of life." [32](And those are the words which I spake unto my servant Moses. And they are true, even as I will, and I have spoken them unto you. See thou show them unto no man until I command you, except them that believe. Amen.)

Moses 5

[1]And it came to pass that after I, the Lord God, had driven them out, that Adam began to till the earth and to have dominion over all the beasts of the field and to eat his bread by the sweat of the brow as I, the Lord, had commanded him. And Eve also, his wife, did labor with him. [2]And Adam knew his wife, and she bare unto him sons and daughters. And they began to multiply and to replenish the earth. [3]And from that time forth, the sons and daughters of Adam began to divide two and two in the land and to till the land and to tend flocks. And they also begat sons and daughters. [4]And Adam called upon the name of the Lord, and Eve also, his wife. And they heard the voice of the Lord from the way towards the Garden of Eden, speaking unto them. And they saw him not, for they were shut out from his presence. [5]And he gave unto them commandment that they should worship the Lord their God and should offer the firstlings of their flocks for an offering unto the Lord. And Adam was obedient unto the commandments of the Lord. [6]And after many days, an angel of the Lord appeared unto Adam, saying: "Why dost thou offer sacrifices unto the

Lord?" And Adam said unto him: "I know not, save the Lord commanded me." ⁷And then the angel spake, saying: "This thing is a similitude of the sacrifice of the Only Begotten of the Father, which is full of grace and truth. ⁸Wherefore, thou shalt do all that thou doest in the name of the Son. And thou shalt repent and call upon God, in the name of the Son, forevermore." ⁹And in that day, the Holy Ghost fell upon Adam, which bore record of the Father and the Son, saying: "I am the Only Begotten of the Father from the beginning, henceforth, and forever; that as thou hast fallen, thou mayest be redeemed, and all mankind, even as many as will." ¹⁰And in that day, Adam blessed God and was filled and began to prophesy concerning all the families of the earth, saying: "Blessed be the name of God, for because of my transgression mine eyes are opened. And in this life I shall have joy, and again in my flesh I shall see God." ¹¹And Eve, his wife, heard all these things and was glad, saying: "Were it not for our transgression we should never have had seed and should never have known good and evil, and the joy of our redemption, and the eternal life which God giveth unto all the obedient." ¹²And Adam and Eve blessed the name of God, and they made all things known unto their sons and their daughters. ¹³And Satan came also among them, saying: "I am also a son of God." And he commanded them, saying: "Believe not." And they believed not and loved Satan more than God. And men began from that time forth to be carnal, sensual, and devilish. ¹⁴And the Lord God called upon men by the Holy Ghost everywhere and commanded them that they should repent. ¹⁵And as many as believed in the Son and repented of their sins should be saved, and as many as believed not and repented not should be damned. And the words went forth out of the mouth of God in a firm decree. Wherefore, they must be fulfilled. ¹⁶And Adam ceased not to call upon God, and Eve also, his wife. And Adam knew Eve, his wife, and she conceived and bare Cain and said: "I have gotten a man from the Lord. Wherefore, he may not reject his words." But behold, also Cain hearkened not, saying: "Who is the Lord, that I should know him?" ¹⁷And she again conceived and bare his brother Abel. And Abel hearkened unto the voice of the Lord. And Abel was a keeper of sheep, but Cain was a tiller of the ground. ¹⁸And Cain loved Satan more than God. And Satan commanded him, saying: "Make an offering unto the Lord." ¹⁹And in process of time, it came to pass that Cain brought of the fruit of the ground an offering unto the Lord. [20]And Abel, he also brought of the firstlings of his flock and of the fat thereof. And the Lord had respect unto Abel and to his offering. [21]But unto Cain and to his offering he had not respect. Now Satan knew this, and it pleased him. And Cain was very wroth, and his countenance fell. [22]And the Lord said unto Cain: "Why art thou wroth? Why is thy countenance fallen? [23]If thou doest well, shalt thou not be accepted? And if thou doest not well, sin lieth at the door. And Satan desireth to have thee. And except thou shalt hearken unto my commandments, I will deliver thee up, and it shall be unto thee according to his desire. And thou shalt rule over him, [24]for from this time forth thou shalt be the father of his lies. Thou shalt be called Perdition, for thou wast also before the world. [25]And it shall be said in times to come that these abominations were had from Cain, for he rejected the greater counsel which was had from God. And this is a cursing which I will put upon thee, except thou repent." [26]And Cain was wroth and listened not anymore to the voice of the Lord, neither to Abel, his brother, who walked in holiness before the Lord. [27]And Adam also, and his wife, mourned before the Lord because of Cain and his brethren. [28]And it came to pass that Cain took one of his brother's daughters to wife, and they loved Satan more than God. [29]And Satan saith unto Cain: "Swear unto me by thy throat, and if thou tell it thou shalt die. And swear thy brethren by their heads and by the living God that they tell it not, for if they tell it they shall surely die, and this that thy father may not know it. And this day I will deliver thy brother Abel into thine hands." [30]And Satan swore unto Cain that he would do according to his commands. And all these things were done in secret. [31]And Cain saith: "Truly I am Mahon, the master of this great secret, that I may murder and get gain." Wherefore, Cain was called Master Mahon, and he gloried in his wickedness. [32]And Cain went into the field, and Cain talked with Abel, his brother. And it came to pass that while they were in the field, Cain rose up against Abel, his brother, and slew him. [33]And Cain gloried in that which he had done, saying: "I am free; surely the flocks of my brother fall into my hands." [34]And the Lord said unto Cain: "Where is Abel, thy brother?" And he said: "I know not; am I my brother's keeper?" [35]And he said: "What hast thou done? The voice of thy brother's blood cries unto me from the ground. [36]And now thou shalt be cursed from the earth, which hath opened her mouth to receive thy brother's blood from thy hand. [37]When thou tillest the ground, it shall not henceforth yield unto thee her strength. A fugitive and a vagabond shalt thou be in the earth." [38]And Cain said unto the Lord: "Satan tempted me because of my brother's flock. And I was wroth also, for his offering thou didst accept and not mine. My punishment is greater than I can bear. [39]Behold, thou hast driven me out this day from the face of the Lord, and from thy face shall I be hid, and I shall be a fugitive and a vagabond in the earth. And it shall come to pass that he that findeth me shall slay me because of mine iniquities, for these things are not hid from the Lord." [40]And I, the Lord, said unto him: "Whosoever slayeth thee, vengeance shall be taken on him sevenfold." And I, the Lord, set a mark upon Cain lest any finding him should kill him. [41]And Cain was shut out from the presence of the Lord, and his wife and many of his brethren, and dwelt in the land of Nod on the east of Eden. [42]And Cain knew his wife, and she conceived and bare Enoch. And he also begat many sons and daughters. And he builded a city, and he called the name of the city after the name of his son Enoch. [43]And unto Enoch was born Irad, and other sons and daughters. And Irad begat Mahujael, and other sons and daughters. And Mahujael begat Mathusael, and other sons and daughters. And Mathusael begat Lamech. [44]And Lamech took unto himself two wives, the name of one being Adah and the name of the other Zillah. [45]And Adah bare Jabal. He was the father of such as dwell in tents, and they were keepers of cattle. And his brother's name was Jubal, who was the father of all such as handle the harp and organ. [46]And Zillah, she also bare Tubal-cain, an instructor of every artificer in brass and iron. And the sister of Tubal-cain was called Naamah. [47]And Lamech said unto his wives: "Adah and Zillah, hear my voice; ye wives of Lamech, hearken unto my speech. For I have slain a man to my wounding, and a young man to my hurt. [48]If Cain shall be avenged sevenfold, truly Lamech shall be seventy and sevenfold." [49]For Lamech, having entered into a covenant with Satan after the manner of Cain, wherein he became Master Mahon, master of that great secret which was administered unto Cain by Satan—and Irad, the son of Enoch, having known their secret, began to reveal it unto the sons of Adam. [50]Wherefore, Lamech, being angry, slew him—not like unto Cain his brother Abel for the sake of getting gain, but he slew him for the oath's sake. [51]For from the days of Cain there was a secret combination, and their works were in the dark, and they knew every man his brother. [52]Wherefore, the Lord cursed Lamech and his house and all them that had covenanted with Satan, for they kept not the commandments of God. And it displeased God, and he ministered not unto them. And their works were abominations and began to spread among all the sons of men. And it was among the sons of men. [53]And among the daughters of men these things were not spoken, because that Lamech had spoken the secret unto his wives, and they rebelled against him and declared these things abroad and had not compassion. [54]Wherefore, Lamech was despised and cast out and came not among the sons of men, lest he should die. [55]And thus the works of darkness began to prevail among all the sons of men. [56]And God cursed the earth with a sore curse and was angry with the wicked, with all the sons of men whom he had made. [57]For they would not hearken unto his voice nor believe on his Only Begotten Son, even him who he declared should come in the meridian of time, who was prepared from before the foundation of the world. [58]And thus the gospel began to be preached from the beginning, being declared by holy angels sent forth from the presence of God, and by his own voice, and by the gift of the Holy Ghost. [59]And thus all things were confirmed unto Adam by an holy ordinance, and the gospel preached and a decree sent forth that it should be in the world until the end thereof. And thus it was. Amen.

MOSES 6

[1]And Adam hearkened unto the voice of God and called upon his sons to repent. [2]And Adam knew his wife again, and she bare a son, and he called his name Seth. And Adam glorified the name of God, for he said: "God hath appointed me another seed instead of Abel, whom Cain slew." [3]And God revealed himself unto Seth, and he rebelled not but offered an acceptable sacrifice like unto his brother Abel. And to him also was born a son, and he called his name Enos. [4]And then began these men to call upon the name of the Lord, and the Lord blessed them. [5]And a book of remembrance was kept in the which was recorded in the language of Adam. For it was given unto as many as called upon God to write by the

spirit of inspiration. ⁶And by them their children were taught to read and write, having a language which was pure and undefiled. ⁷"Now this same priesthood which was in the beginning shall be in the end of the world also." ⁸Now this prophecy Adam spake as he was moved upon. And a genealogy was kept of the children of God. And this was the book of the generations of Adam, saying: "In the day that God created man, in the likeness of God made he him, ⁹in the image of his own body. Male and female created he them and blessed them and called their name Adam, in the day when they were created and became living souls in the land, upon the footstool of God." ¹⁰And Adam lived one hundred and thirty years and begat a son, in his own likeness after his image, and called his name Seth. ¹¹And the days of Adam after he had begotten Seth were eight hundred seventy years. And he begat many sons and daughters. ¹²And all the days that Adam lived were one thousand years, and he died. ¹³Seth lived one hundred and five years and begat Enos, and prophesied in all his days, and taught Enos in the ways of God. Wherefore, Enos prophesied also. ¹⁴And Seth lived after he begat Enos eight hundred seventy-six years and begat many sons and daughters. ¹⁵And the children of men were numerous upon all the face of the land. And in these days, Satan had great dominion among men and raged in their hearts. And from thenceforth came wars and bloodsheds, and a man's hand was against his own brother in administering death, because of secret works, seeking for power. ¹⁶And all the days of Seth were nine hundred eighty-one years, and he died. ¹⁷And Enos lived ninety years and begat Cainan. And Enos and the residue of the people of God came out from the land which was called Shulon and dwelt in a land of promise, which he called after his own son whom he had named Cainan, whom he begat when he was ninety years old. ¹⁸And Enos lived after he begat Cainan eight hundred fifty years and begat many sons and daughters. And all the days of Enos were nine hundred forty years, and he died. ¹⁹And Cainan lived one hundred seventeen years and begat Mahalaleel. And Cainan lived after he begat Mahalaleel eight hundred and forty and begat sons and daughters. And all the days of Cainan were nine hundred fifty-seven years, and he died. ²⁰And Mahalaleel lived one hundred fifteen years and begat Jared. And Mahalaleel lived after he begat Jared eight hundred and thirty years and begat sons and daughters. And all the days of Mahalaleel were nine hundred forty-five, and he died. ²¹And Jared lived a hundred and sixty and two years and begat Enoch. And Jared lived after he begat Enoch eight hundred years and begat sons and daughters. And Jared taught Enoch in all the ways of God. ²²And this is the genealogy of the sons of Adam, who was the son of God with whom God himself conversed. ²³And they were preachers of righteousness and spake, and prophesied, and called upon all men everywhere to repent. And faith was taught unto the children of men. ²⁴And it came to pass that all the days of Jared were nine hundred sixty and two years, and he died. ²⁵And Enoch lived sixty and five years and begat Methuselah. ²⁶And it came to pass that Enoch journeyed in the land among the people. And as he journeyed, the Spirit of God descended out of heaven and abode upon him. ²⁷And he heard a voice from heaven, saying: "Enoch, my son, prophesy unto this people, and say unto them: 'Repent.' For thus saith the Lord: I am angry with this people, and my fierce anger is kindled against them. For their hearts have waxed hard, and their ears are dull of hearing, and their eyes cannot see afar off. ²⁸And for these many generations, even since the day that I created them, have they gone astray and have denied me and have sought their own counsels in the dark. And in their own abominations have they devised murder and have not kept the commandment which I gave unto their father Adam. ²⁹Wherefore, they have forsworn themselves, and by their oaths they have brought upon themselves death. And an hell I have prepared for them if they repent not. ³⁰And this is a decree which I have sent forth in the beginning of the world, from mine own mouth, from the foundation thereof. And by the mouths of my servants, thy fathers, have I decreed it, even as it shall be sent forth in the world unto the end thereof." ³¹And when Enoch had heard these words, he bowed himself to the earth before the Lord and spake before the Lord, saying: "Why is it that I have found favor in thy sight and am but a lad, and all the people hate me for I am slow of speech? Wherefore am I thy servant?" ³²And the Lord said unto Enoch: "Go forth and do as I have commanded thee, and no man shall pierce thee. Open thy mouth, and it shall be filled. I will give thee utterance. For all flesh is in my hands, and I will do as seemeth me good. ³³Say unto this people: 'Choose ye this day to serve the Lord God who made you.' ³⁴Behold, my Spirit is upon you. Wherefore, all thy words will I justify. And the mountains shall flee before you, and the rivers shall turn from their course. And thou shalt abide in me and I in you. Therefore, walk with me." [35]And the Lord spake unto Enoch and said unto him: "Anoint thine eyes with clay and wash them, and thou shalt see." And he did so. [36]And he beheld the spirits that God had created, and he beheld also things which were not visible. And from thenceforth came the saying abroad in the land, "A seer hath the Lord raised up unto his people." [37]And it came to pass that Enoch went forth in the land among the people—standing upon the hills and the high places—and cried with a loud voice, testifying against their works. And all men were offended because of him. [38]And they came forth to hear him upon the high places, saying unto the tent keepers: "Tarry ye here and keep the tents while we go yonder to behold the seer, for he prophesieth. And there is a strange thing in the land, a wild man hath come among us." [39]And it came to pass, when they heard him, no man laid his hands on him. For fear came on all them that heard him, for he walked with God. [40]And there came a man unto him whose name was Mahijah, and said unto him: "Tell us plainly who thou art and from whence thou camest." [41]And he saith unto them: "I came out from the land of Cainan, the land of my fathers, a land of righteousness unto this day. And my father taught me in all the ways of God. [42]And it came to pass, as I journeyed from the land of Cainan, by the sea east, I beheld a vision. And lo, the heavens I saw. And the Lord spake with me and gave me commandment. Wherefore, for this cause, to keep the commandment, I speak forth these words." [43]And Enoch continued his speech, saying: "The Lord which spake with me, the same is the God of heaven, and he is my God and your God, and ye are my brethren. And why counsel ye yourselves and deny the God of heaven? [44]The heavens hath he made, the earth is his footstool, and the foundation thereof is his. Behold, he laid it, and hosts of men hath he brought in upon the face thereof. [45]And death hath come upon our fathers. Nevertheless, we know them and cannot deny. And even the first of all we know, even Adam. [46]For a book of remembrance we have written among us, according to the pattern given by the finger of God. And it is given in our own language." [47]And as Enoch spake forth the words of God, the people trembled and could not stand before his presence. [48]And he said unto them: "Because that Adam fell we are, and by his fall came death, and we are made partakers of misery and woe. [49]Behold, Satan hath come among the children of men and tempteth them to worship him. And men have become carnal, sensual, and devilish and are shut out from the presence of God. ⁵⁰But God hath made known unto my fathers that all men must repent. ⁵¹And he called upon our father Adam by his own voice, saying: 'I am God. I made the world and men before they were in the flesh.' ⁵²And he also said unto him: 'If thou wilt turn unto me and hearken unto my voice and believe, and repent of all thy transgressions and be baptized, even in water in the name of mine Only Begotten Son, who is full of grace and truth, who is Jesus Christ—the only name which shall be given under heaven whereby salvation shall come unto the children of men—and ye shall receive the gift of the holy Ghost, asking all things in his name. And whatsoever ye shall ask, it shall be given you.' ⁵³And our father Adam spake unto the Lord and said: 'Why is it that men must repent and be baptized in water?' And the Lord said unto Adam: 'Behold, I have forgiven thee thy transgressions in the garden of Eden.' ⁵⁴Hence came the saying abroad among the people that the Son of God hath atoned for original guilt, wherein the sins of the parents cannot be answered upon the heads of the children, for they are whole from the foundation of the world. ⁵⁵And the Lord spake unto Adam, saying: 'Inasmuch as thy children are conceived in sin, even so when they begin to grow up, sin conceiveth in their hearts, and they taste the bitter that they may know to prize the good. ⁵⁶And it is given unto them to know good from evil. Wherefore, they are agents unto themselves. And I have given unto you another law and commandment. ⁵⁷Wherefore, teach it unto your children, that all men everywhere must repent, or they can in no wise inherit the kingdom of God. For no unclean thing can dwell there or dwell in his presence. For in the language of Adam, Man of Holiness is his name. And the name of his Only Begotten is the Son—a man, a righteous judge who shall come in the meridian of time. ⁵⁸Therefore, I give unto you a commandment to teach these things freely unto your children, saying ⁵⁹that by reason of transgression cometh the fall, which fall bringeth death. And inasmuch as they were born into the world by water, and blood, and the spirit which I have made—and so became of dust a living soul—even so ye must be born again into the kingdom of heaven of water, and of the Spirit, and be cleansed by blood—even the blood of mine Only Begotten—that ye may be sanctified from all sin and enjoy the words of eternal life in this world and eternal life in the world to come, even immortal glory. ⁶⁰For by the water ye keep the commandment, by the Spirit ye are justified, and by the blood ye are sanctified. ⁶¹Therefore, it is given to abide in you the record of heaven, the Comforter, the keys of the kingdom of heaven, the truth of all things, that which quickeneth all things, which maketh alive all things, that which knoweth all things and hath all power according to wisdom, mercy, truth, justice, and judgment. ⁶²And now behold, I say unto you: This is the plan of salvation unto all men through the blood of mine Only Begotten, which shall come in the meridian of time. ⁶³And behold, all things have their likeness, and all things are created and made to bear record of me— both things which are temporal and things which are spiritual, things which are in the heavens above and things which are on the earth, and things which are in the earth and things which are under the earth. Both above and beneath, all things bear record of me.' ⁶⁴And it came to pass, when the Lord had spoken with Adam, our father, that Adam cried unto the Lord, and he was caught away by the Spirit of the Lord and was carried down into the water, and was laid under the water, and was brought forth out of the water. ⁶⁵And thus he was baptized, and the Spirit of God descended upon him. And thus he was born of the Spirit and became quickened in the inner man. ⁶⁶And he heard a voice out of heaven, saying: 'Thou art baptized with fire and with the Holy Ghost. This is the record of the Father and the Son, from henceforth and forever. ⁶⁷And thou art after the order of him who was without beginning of days or end of years, from all eternity to all eternity. ⁶⁸Behold, thou art one in me, a son of God. And thus may all become my sons. Amen.'"

MOSES 7

¹And it came to pass that Enoch continued his speech, saying: "Behold, our father Adam taught these things, and many have believed and become the sons of God. And many have believed not and have perished in their sins and are looking forth, with fear in torment, for the fiery indignation of the wrath of God to be poured out upon them." ²And from that time forth, Enoch began to prophesy, saying unto the people that: "As I was

journeying and stood in the place Mahujah and cried unto the Lord, there came a voice out of heaven, saying: 'Turn ye and get ye upon the mount Simeon.' ³And it came to pass that I turned and went upon the mount. And as I stood upon the mount, I beheld the heavens open, and I was clothed upon with glory. ⁴And I saw the Lord. He stood before my face, and he talked with me, even as a man talketh one with another, face to face. And he saith unto me: 'Look, and I will show unto thee the world for the space of many generations.' ⁵And it came to pass that I beheld in the valley of Shum, and lo, a great people which dwelt in tents, which were the people of Shum. ⁶And again the Lord said unto me: 'Look.' And I looked towards the north, and I beheld the people of Canaan, which dwelt in tents. ⁷And the Lord said unto me: 'Prophesy.' And I prophesied, saying: 'Behold, the people of Canaan, which are numerous, shall go forth in battle array against the people of Shum and shall slay them, that they shall utterly be destroyed. And the people of Canaan shall divide themselves in the land, and the land shall be barren and unfruitful. And none other people shall dwell there but the people of Canaan. ⁸For behold, the Lord shall curse the land with much heat, and the barrenness thereof shall go forth forever.' And there was a blackness come upon all the children of Canaan, that they were despised among all people. ⁹And it came to pass, the Lord said unto me: 'Look.' And I looked, and I beheld the land of Sharon, and the land of Enoch, and the land of Omner, and the land of Heni, and the land of Shem, and the land of Haner, and the land of Hanannihah, and all the inhabitants thereof. ¹⁰And the Lord said unto me: 'Go forth to this people, and say unto them: "Repent," lest I come out and smite them with a curse, and they die.' ¹¹And he gave unto me a commandment that I should baptize in the name of the Father, and of the Son, which is full of grace and truth, and the Holy Ghost, which beareth record of the Father and the Son." ¹²And it came to pass that Enoch continued to call upon all the people, save it were the people of Canaan, to repent. ¹³And so great was the faith of Enoch that he led the people of God. And their enemies came to battle against them. And he spake the word of the Lord, and the earth trembled and the mountains fled, even according to his command, and the rivers of water were turned out of their course, and the roar of the lions was heard out of the wilderness. And all nations feared greatly, so powerful was the word of Enoch and so great was the power of the language which God had given him. [14]There also came up a land out of the depths of the sea. And so great was the fear of the enemies of the people of God that they fled and stood afar off and went upon the land which came up out of the depths of the sea. [15]And the giants of the land also stood afar off. And there went forth a curse upon all the people which fought against God. [16]And from that time forth, there were wars and bloodsheds among them. But the Lord came and dwelt with his people, and they dwelt in righteousness. [17]The fear of the Lord was upon all nations, so great was the glory of the Lord which was upon his people. And the Lord blessed the land, and they were blessed upon the mountains and upon the high places and did flourish. [18]And the Lord called his people Zion, because they were of one heart, and of one mind, and dwelt in righteousness, and there were no poor among them. [19]And Enoch continued his preaching in righteousness unto the people of God. And it came to pass in his days that he built a city that was called the City of Holiness, even Zion. [20]And it came to pass that Enoch talked with the Lord, and he said unto the Lord: "Surely, Zion shall dwell in safety forever." And the Lord said unto Enoch: "Zion have I blessed, but the residue of the people have I cursed." [21]And it came to pass that the Lord showed unto Enoch all the inhabitants of the earth. And he beheld, and lo, Zion in process of time was taken up into heaven. And the Lord said unto Enoch: "Behold mine abode forever." [22]And Enoch also beheld the residue of the people which were the sons of Adam. And they were a mixture of all the seed of Adam, save it were the seed of Cain. For the seed of Cain were black and had not place among them. [23]And after that Zion was taken up into heaven, Enoch beheld, and lo, all the nations of the earth were before him. [24]And there came generation upon generation. And Enoch was high and lifted up, even in the bosom of the Father and the Son of Man. And behold, the powers of Satan were upon all the face of the earth. [25]And he saw angels descending out of heaven. And he heard a loud voice, saying: "Woe, woe be unto the inhabitants of the earth." [26]And he beheld Satan, and he had a great chain in his hand. And he veiled the whole face of the earth with darkness. And he looked up and laughed, and his angels rejoiced. [27]And Enoch beheld angels descending out of heaven, bearing testimony of the Father and Son. And the Holy Ghost fell on many, and they were caught up by the powers of heaven into Zion. ²⁸And it came to pass that Enoch looked upon the residue of the people, and he wept. And he beheld, and lo, the heavens wept also and shed forth their tears as the rain upon the mountains. ²⁹And Enoch said unto the heavens: "How is it that thou canst weep, seeing thou art holy and from all eternity to all eternity? ³⁰And were it possible that man could number the particles of the earth, yea and millions of earths like this, it would not be a beginning to the number of thy creations. And thy curtains are stretched out still. And thou art there, and thy presence is there. And also thou art just; thou art merciful and kind forever. ³¹Thou hast taken Zion to thine own bosom from all thy creations, from all eternity to all eternity. Naught but peace, justice, and truth is the habitation of thy throne, and mercy shall go before thy face and have no end. How is it that thou canst weep?" ³²The Lord said unto Enoch: "Behold, these thy brethren, they are the workmanship of mine own hands. And I gave unto them their intelligence. And in the Garden of Eden, man had agency. ³³And unto thy brethren have I said, and also given commandment, that they should love one another and that they should serve me their God. But behold, they are without affection, and they hate their own blood. ³⁴And the fire of mine indignation is kindled against them, and in my hot displeasure will I send in the floods upon them, for my fierce anger is kindled against them. ³⁵Behold, I am God. Man of Holiness is my name, Man of Council is my name, and Endless and Eternal is my name also. ³⁶Wherefore, I can stretch forth mine hands and hold all the creations which I have made. And mine eye can pierce them also. And among all the workmanship of mine hand, there has not been so great wickedness as among thy brethren. ³⁷But behold, their sins shall be upon the heads of their fathers. Satan shall be their master, and misery shall be their doom. And the whole heavens shall weep over them, even all the workmanship of mine hands. Wherefore, should not the heavens weep, seeing these shall suffer? ³⁸But behold, these which thine eyes are upon shall perish in the floods. And behold, I will shut them up; a prison have I prepared for them. ³⁹And he whom I have chosen has pled before my face. Wherefore, he suffereth for their sins inasmuch as they will repent, in the day that my Chosen shall return unto me. And until that day, they shall be in torment. ⁴⁰Wherefore, for this shall the heaven weep, yea, and all the workmanship of mine hands." ⁴¹And it came to pass that the Lord spake unto Enoch and told Enoch all the doings of the children of men. Wherefore, Enoch knew and looked upon their wickedness and their misery and wept and stretched forth his arms. And he beheld eternity, and his bowels yearned, and all eternity shook. ⁴²And Enoch saw Noah also and his family, that the posterity of all the sons of Noah should be saved with a temporal salvation. ⁴³Wherefore, Enoch saw that Noah built an ark, and the Lord smiled upon it and held it in his own hand. But upon the residue of the wicked came the floods and swallowed them up. ⁴⁴And as Enoch saw thus, he had bitterness of soul and wept over his brethren and said unto the heavens: "I will refuse to be comforted." But the Lord said unto Enoch: "Lift up your heart and be glad, and look." ⁴⁵And it came to pass that Enoch looked. And from Noah he beheld all the families of the earth. And he cried unto the Lord, saying: "When shall the day of the Lord come? When shall the blood of the Righteous be shed that all they that mourn may be sanctified and have eternal life?" ⁴⁶And the Lord said: "It shall be in the meridian of time, in the days of wickedness and vengeance." ⁴⁷And behold, Enoch saw the day of the coming of the Son of Man, even in the flesh. And his soul rejoiced, saying: "The Righteous is lifted up, and the Lamb is slain from the foundation of the world. And through faith I am in the bosom of the Father. And behold, Zion is with me." ⁴⁸And it came to pass that Enoch looked upon the earth. And he heard a voice from the bowels thereof, saying: "Woe, woe is me, the mother of men. I am pained; I am weary because of the wickedness of my children. When shall I rest and be cleansed from the filthiness which has gone forth out of me? When will my Creator sanctify me that I may rest, and righteousness for a season abide upon my face?" ⁴⁹And when Enoch heard the earth mourn, he wept and cried unto the Lord, saying: "O Lord, wilt thou not have compassion upon the earth? Wilt thou not bless the children of Noah?" ⁵⁰And it came to pass that Enoch continued his cry unto the Lord, saying: "I ask thee, O Lord, in the name of thine Only Begotten, that thou wilt have mercy upon Noah and his seed, that the earth might never more be covered by the floods." ⁵¹And the Lord could not withhold. And he covenanted with Enoch and sware unto him with an oath that he would stay the floods, that he would call upon the children of Noah. ⁵²And he sent forth an unalterable decree that from a remnant of his seed should come all nations while the earth should stand. ⁵³And the Lord said: "Blessed is he through whose seed Messiah shall come." For he saith: "I am Messiah, the King of Zion, the Rock of heaven, which is broad as eternity. And whoso cometh in at the gate and climbeth up by me shall never fall. Wherefore, blessed are they of whom I have spoken, for they shall come forth with songs of everlasting joy." [54]And it came to pass that Enoch cried unto the Lord, saying: "When the Son of Man cometh in the flesh, shall the earth rest? I pray thee, show me these things." [55]And the Lord said unto Enoch: "Look." And he looked and beheld the Son of Man lifted upon the cross, after the manner of men. [56]And he heard a loud voice, and the heavens were veiled, and all the creation of God mourned. And the earth groaned, and the rocks were rent, and the Saints arose and were crowned at the right hand of the Son of Man with crowns of glory. [57]And as many of the spirits as were in prison came forth and stood on the right hand of God. And the remainder were reserved in chains of darkness until the judgment of the great day. [58]And Enoch wept and cried unto the Lord again, saying: "When shall the earth rest?" [59]And Enoch beheld the Son of Man ascend up unto the Father. And he called unto the Lord, saying: "Wilt thou not come again upon the earth? For inasmuch as thou art God, and I know thee, and thou hast sworn unto me and commanded me that I should ask in the name of thine Only Begotten—thou hast made me and given unto me a right to thy throne, and not of myself but through thine own grace—wherefore, I ask thee if thou wilt not come again on the earth." [60]And the Lord said unto Enoch: "As I live, even so will I come in the last days, in the days of wickedness and vengeance, to fulfill the oath which I have made unto you concerning the children of Noah. [61]And the day shall come that the earth shall rest. But before that day, the heavens shall be darkened, and a veil of darkness shall cover the earth. And the heavens shall shake and also the earth. And great tribulations shall be among the children of men, but my people will I preserve. [62]And righteousness will I send down out of heaven. Truth will I send forth out of the earth, to bear testimony of mine Only Begotten, his resurrection from the dead, yea, and also the resurrection of all men. And righteousness and truth will I cause to sweep the earth as with the flood, to gather out mine own elect from the four quarters of the earth unto a place which I shall prepare—an holy city—that my people may gird up their loins and be looking forth for the time of my coming. For there shall be my tabernacle, and it shall be called Zion, a New Jerusalem." [63]And the Lord said unto Enoch: "Then shalt thou and all thy city meet them there. And we will receive them into our bosom, and they shall see us. And we will fall upon their necks, and they shall fall upon our necks, and we will kiss each other. [64]And there shall be mine abode. And it shall be Zion, which shall come forth out of all the creations which I have made. And for the space of a thousand years shall the earth rest." [65]And it came to pass that Enoch saw the day of the coming of the Son of Man, in the last days, to dwell on the earth in right-eousness for the space of a thousand years. [66]But before that day, he saw great tribulation among the wicked. And he also saw the sea, that it was troubled, and men's hearts failing them, looking forth with fear for the judgments of the Almighty God which should come upon the wicked. [67]And the Lord showed Enoch all things, even unto the end of the world. And he saw the day of the righteous, the hour of their redemption, and received a fullness of joy. [68]And all the days of Zion, in the days of Enoch, were three hundred and sixty-five years. [69]And Enoch and all his people walked with God. And he dwelt in the midst of Zion. And it came to pass that Zion was not, for God received it up into his own bosom. And from thence went forth the saying, "Zion is fled."

MOSES 8

[1]And all the days of Enoch were four hundred thirty years. [2]And it came to pass that Methuselah, the son of Enoch, was not taken, that the covenants of the Lord might be fulfilled which he made to Enoch. For he truly covenanted with Enoch that Noah should be of the fruit of his loins. [3]And it came to pass that Methuselah prophesied that from his loins should spring all the kingdoms of the earth (through Noah). And he took glory unto himself. [4]And there came forth a great famine into the land. And the Lord cursed the earth with a sore curse. And many of the inhabi-tants thereof died. [5]And it came to pass that Methuselah lived two hun-dred eighteen years and begat Lamech. [6]And Methuselah lived after he begat Lamech seven hundred eighty and two years and begat sons and daughters. [7]And all the days of Methuselah were one thousand years, and

he died. [8]And Lamech lived an hundred eighty and two years and begat a son. [9]And he called his name Noah, saying: "This son shall comfort us concerning our work and toil of our hands, because of the ground which the Lord hath cursed." [10]And Lamech lived after he begat Noah five hundred ninety and five years and begat sons and daughters. [11]And all the days of Lamech were seven hundred seventy and seven years, and he died. [12]And Noah was four hundred and fifty years old and begat Japheth. And forty-two years afterward, he begat Shem of her who was the mother of Japheth. And when he was five hundred years old, he begat Ham. [13]And Noah and his sons hearkened unto the Lord and gave heed, and they were called the sons of God. [14]And when these men began to multiply on the face of the earth, and daughters were born unto them, that the sons of men saw that their daughters were fair. They took them wives, even as they chose. [15]And the Lord said unto Noah: "The daughters of thy sons have sold themselves. For behold, mine anger is kindled against the sons of men, for they will not hearken to my voice." [16]And it came to pass that Noah prophesied and taught the things of God, even as it was in the beginning. [17]And the Lord said unto Noah: "My spirit shall not always strive with man, for he shall know that all flesh shall die. Yet his days shall be an hundred and twenty years. And if men do not repent, I will send in the floods upon them." [18]And in those days there were giants on the earth. And they sought Noah to take away his life. But the Lord was with Noah, and the power of the Lord was upon him. [19]And the Lord ordained Noah after his own order and commanded him that he should go forth and declare his gospel unto the children of men, even as it was given unto Enoch. [20]And it came to pass that Noah called upon men that they should repent, but they hearkened not unto his words. [21]And also, after that they had heard him, they came up before him, saying: "Behold, we are the sons of God. Have we not taken unto ourselves the daughters of men? And are we not eating and drinking and marrying and given in marriage? And our wives bear unto us children, and the same are mighty men which are like unto them of old—men of great renown." And they hearkened not unto the words of Noah. [22]And God saw that the wickedness of man had become great in the earth. And every man was lifted up in the imagination of the thoughts of his heart, being only evil continually. [23]And it came to pass that Noah continued his preaching unto the people, saying:

"Hearken and give heed unto my words. [24]Believe and repent of your sins, and be baptized in the name of Jesus Christ, the Son of God, even as our fathers did. And ye shall receive the gift of the Holy Ghost, that ye may have all things made manifest. And if you do not do this, the floods will come in upon you." Nevertheless, they hearkened not. [25]And it repented Noah, and his heart was pained, that the Lord had made man on the earth. And it grieved him at his heart. [26]And the Lord said: "I will destroy man, whom I have created, from the face of the earth—both man, and beast, and the creeping things, and the fowls of the air. For it repenteth Noah that I have created them and that I have made them. And he hath called upon me, for they have sought his life." [27]And thus Noah found grace in the eyes of the Lord, for Noah was a just man and perfect in his generations. And he walked with God, and also his three sons—Shem, Ham, and Japheth. [28]But the earth was corrupt before God; it was filled with violence. [29]And God looked upon it, and behold, it was corrupt, for all flesh had corrupted its way upon the earth. [30]And God said unto Noah: "The end of all flesh is come before me, for the earth is filled with violence. And behold, I will destroy all flesh from off the earth."

AN APPRECIATION

C oncerning a time of persecution of the early Saints in June 1830, Joseph Smith's history records: "Amid all the trials and tribulations we had to wade through, the Lord, who well knew our infantile and delicate situation, vouchsafed for us a supply of strength, and granted us 'line upon line of knowledge—here a little and there a little,' of which the following was a precious morsel."[1] What was revealed is now known as Moses chapter 1, the beginning of the Book of Moses and the beginning also of the Joseph Smith Translation of the Bible.

Indeed Moses 1 is a "precious morsel," and the same can be said for all of the Book of Moses. The Book of Moses plays a special role in the restoration of the fulness of the gospel. It may well be that it contains more distinctively Latter-day Saint doctrine than any other comparable section of scripture. Consider the following topics, in which profound truths, significant to our gospel understanding, are revealed: Man is indeed in the image of God (see Moses 6:9), and God speaks with His prophets as one man speaks with another—"face to face" (Moses 7:4). The Father's work is without end, and His worlds are "without number" (Moses 1:33). In all of His creations, His work and glory consist of bringing to pass the immortality and eternal life of His children (see Moses 1:39; see also 1:33–39). Jesus Christ was with the Father in the beginning, He cast Satan out for rebellion in the premortal world (see Moses 4:2–3), and He was the Creator of this world as well as of all the Father's innumerable worlds (see Moses 1:33).

---

1. Joseph Smith, *History of the Church of Jesus Christ of Latter-day Saints*, ed. B. H. Roberts, 2nd ed. rev. (Salt Lake City: Deseret Book, 1957), 1:98.

Jesus Christ is the only name given under heaven by which we can be saved (see Moses 6:52). Redemption is through His blood (see Moses 6:62), and animal sacrifice is in similitude of His sinless offering (see Moses 5:7). Satan stepped forward to take upon himself prerogatives that were not his, rebelling against God and Christ and seeking for himself God's honor, power, and glory. His desire is to destroy our agency and lead us into bondage (see Moses 4:1–4). The fall of our first parents, Adam and Eve, was a necessary part of humanity's course and a blessing for us as individuals. Had they not fallen, they would not have had children, they never would have known good and evil and the joy of redemption, and neither they nor we would ever have an opportunity for eternal life (see Moses 5:10–11). The gospel of Jesus Christ was revealed in the beginning; Adam was a Christian and was baptized in Jesus's name (see Moses 6:51–62, 64–66), Adam and Eve taught the gospel to their children (see Moses 5:9–12), and their descendants believed in Christ, worshiped the Father in His name, and knew and understood the principles and ordinances of the gospel (see Moses 7:10–11; 8:23–24). Moses knew Christ as his Creator and Redeemer (see Moses 1:6, 32–33; 4:1–3), and Enoch established a community of Saints, walked with God, and was translated (see Moses 7:21, 27, 69).

Many of these teachings are found nowhere else in scripture, even in other books of modern revelation. These and other remarkable doctrinal contributions set the Book of Moses apart as a "precious morsel" without peer. It is one of the great treasures of the Restoration and a blessing of inestimable worth to the Church. It is my view that it is also an incontrovertible witness to the calling of Joseph Smith, because no mortal could have produced a work of such profound inspiration, scope, and vision. Whether in handwriting on its original manuscripts or in print in today's modern edition, its truths come forward one after another to bear testimony of the universal scope of Christ's gospel, the redemptive power of His mission, and the divine calling of the Prophet Joseph Smith, who brought this precious record forth.

INDEX